Lifesaver Lessons
SCIENCE
GRADE 5

What Are Lifesaver Lessons®?

Lifesaver Lessons are well-planned, easy-to-implement, curriculum-based lessons. Each lesson contains a complete materials list, step-by-step instructions, a reproducible activity or pattern, and several extension activities.

How Do I Use A Lifesaver Lesson?

Each Lifesaver Lesson is designed to decrease your preparation time and increase the amount of quality teaching time with your students. These lessons are great for introducing or reinforcing new concepts. You may want to look through the lessons to see what types of materials to gather. After completing a lesson, be sure to check out the fun-filled extension activities.

What Materials Will I Need?

Most of the materials for each lesson can be easily found in your classroom or school. Check the list of materials below for any items you may need to gather or purchase.

- transparencies
- transparency markers
- hairpins
- construction paper
- yarn
- scissors
- glue
- index cards
- pipe cleaners
- bag ties
- egg cartons
- tissue paper
- clay
- tape
- crayons
- colored pencils
- drawing paper
- metal rings
- pictures (vertebrates, invertebrates, plants and animals from ecosystems)

- measuring spoons
- measuring cups
- permanent markers
- bucket
- chart paper
- markers
- encyclopedias
- one-quart milk or juice container
- bulletin-board paper
- butcher paper
- 20-ounce plastic soda bottle
- 3 different-sized magnets
- unglazed ceramic tiles
- clean recyclable containers (paper, plastic, aluminum, and glass)
- balloon
- baking soda
- cookie

- knife
- rubber bands
- candle
- wooden matches
- chalk
- white cards
- bar magnets
- iron filings
- paper clips
- pencils
- rulers
- cornstarch or baby powder
- filmstrip projector
- clear drinking glass
- tennis ball
- eraser
- sandwich bags

- waxed paper
- dictionaries
- flat mirrors
- black cards
- flashlights
- pennies
- string
- small paper plates
- shoeboxes
- world map
- pushpins

- water
- rocks
- newspaper
- hammer
- coin
- vinegar
- eyedroppers
- safety goggles
- stapler
- globe
- tagboard
- hole puncher

Project Editor:
Thad H. McLaurin

Writers:
Elizabeth H. Lindsay, Debra Liverman, Thad H. McLaurin,
Cindy Mondello, Stephanie Willett-Smith

Artists:
Cathy Spangler Bruce, Pam Crane, Nick Greenwood, Clevell Harris,
Mary Lester, Barry Slate, Donna K. Teal

Cover Artist:
Jennifer Tipton Bennett

An average animal cell is about one one-thousandth of an inch across.

Table Of Contents

A Method To Your Madness

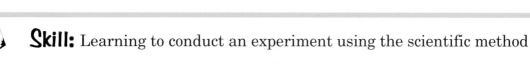

The scientific method is a great way to capture a child's interest in science. After conducting the following hands-on experiments, your class will be "mad" about science.

Skill: Learning to conduct an experiment using the scientific method

Estimated Lesson Time: 45 minutes

Teacher Preparation:
1. Make one copy of page 5 for each pair of students.
2. Make a transparency of page 5.

Materials:
1 blank transparency
1 transparency marker
1 hairpin for each pair of students
1 copy of page 5 for each pair

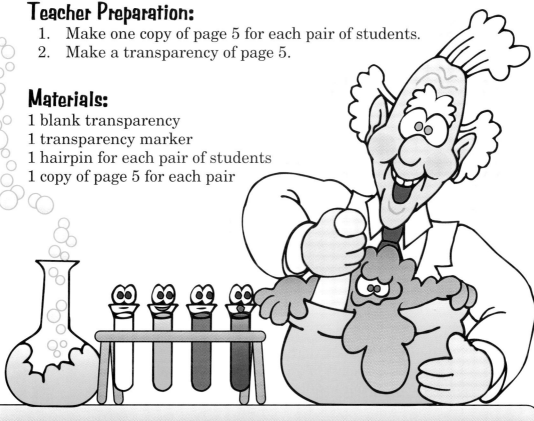

Background Information:
   The *scientific method* is an orderly method used in scientific research. It consists of identifying the experiment's purpose, researching and collecting data, formulating a hypothesis, performing the experiment, observing, interpreting the results, and drawing a conclusion.

Introducing The Lesson:

Ask your students, "In which position—above your head or down by your sides—do you think the veins in your hands will be more visible?" Remind students that you want predictions only.

Steps:

1. Place the transparency of page 5 on the overhead projector. Identify each step of the scientific method. Tell students they will use the scientific method to find an answer to the question above. Have students help you complete the *purpose, hypothesis, materials,* and *procedure* sections of the lab report (transparency).

2. Instruct each student to hold her hands down by her sides for one minute, then observe the veins on the backs of her hands. Continue the experiment by having each student hold her hands over her head for one minute, then observe the veins on the backs of her hands.

3. Record students' *observations* and *conclusion* on the lab report. *(Holding your hands down by your sides causes the blood to fill the veins in your hands before going back to your heart. Holding your hands above your head causes less pressure on the veins, and they seem to disappear.)*

4. Divide students into pairs. Give each pair a copy of page 5 and a hairpin. Instruct each pair to follow the procedure below, then record its data on the lab report.

   A. Instruct your partner to close her eyes. Gently press one or both points of the hairpin on your partner's arm. Ask your partner to tell you if one or two points of the hairpin are touching her skin. Record the response on the back of this paper. Be sure to include how many points you used and if she guessed correctly.

   B. Repeat the process—touching the back of her hand, fingertip, and neck. Record your results.

   C. Try touching her skin in the same places again with the points of the hairpin farther apart. Record your results.

5. Discuss the results of the experiment. *(Skin is more sensitive in places on the body that have more nerve endings. Fingertips have more nerve endings than the back of the hand, the neck, and the arm. Therefore on the back of the hand, neck, and arm, it is impossible to feel if one or two points are touching the skin, unless the points are wide apart.)*

Method To My Madness

Purpose: (Why are you conducting this experiment?) _____

Hypothesis: (What do you think will happen?) _____

Materials: (What items do you need?) _____

Procedure: (What steps will you take to prove or disprove your hypothesis?)

Observations: (What happened?)

Conclusion: (Was your hypothesis correct?)

How To Extend The Lesson:

For more practice on the scientific method, have students conduct the following experiments:

Experiment 1

Purpose: What happens when the air pressure inside an object is not equal to the air pressure outside the object?

Materials: small plastic cup, index card (large enough to cover the opening of the cup), water, tray to catch spills

Procedure:

1. Hold the index card over the mouth of the cup and turn the cup over. Predict what you think will happen if you let go of the index card.
2. Let go of the index card. Observe and record what happens.
3. Fill the cup 1/2 full of water. Hold the index card over the cup by placing your palm over the card. Quickly turn the cup over. Predict what you think will happen if you let go of the index card.
4. Let go of the index card. Observe and record what happens.

(Since the air pressure inside and outside the empty cup is the same, gravity pulls the paper off the cup. In the cup half-filled with water, the air pressure inside and outside the cup starts out the same. When the cup is turned over, the water level in the cup drops. The amount of air pressure inside the cup, above the water, is less than the air pressure outside the cup. The outside air pressure pushes the paper in, holding the water in the cup.)

Experiment 2

Purpose: What happens when surface tension is broken?

Materials: ground black pepper, small bowl, water, liquid soap

Procedure:

1. Fill the bowl with water.
2. Sprinkle pepper on the surface of the water. Where is most of the pepper?
3. Place a drop of liquid soap on the water near the edge of the bowl.
4. Observe and record what happens.

(The pepper flakes fall to the bottom when the liquid soap is added. Adding the liquid soap reduces the lifting power or the surface tension of the water.)

Wide World Of Plants

Familiarize students with the ways scientists classify plants.

Skill: Classifying plants

Estimated Lesson Time: 45 minutes

Teacher Preparation:
Duplicate one copy of page 9 for each pair of students.

Materials:
(for each pair of students)
1 copy of page 9
1 large sheet of construction paper
yarn
scissors
glue

A floating duckweed is the smallest flowering plant. Twenty-five of these plants would fit across your fingernail!

The oldest seed plants are the ancestors of the ginkgo trees. They first appeared in China 180,000,000 years ago when dinosaurs roamed the earth!

Background Information:
- Plants can be divided into two groups—those that reproduce with seeds and those that do not.
- Plants that don't make seeds are *mosses, ferns, fungi,* and *algae.*
- Ferns have roots, stems, and leaves. Mosses, fungi, and algae do not.
- Plants that do make seeds can also be divided into two groups—*angiosperms,* or flowering plants, and *gymnosperms,* or naked seed plants.
- There are two types of angiosperms—*monocots,* those producing seeds with one seed leaf, and *dicots,* those producing seeds with two seed leaves.

Introducing The Lesson:

Ask students to brainstorm the different ways that the class could be divided into two groups.

Steps:

1. Have students stand on one side of the room or the other, according to an *attribute* (a natural characteristic or quality) that you specify. At first, keep the attributes simple; for example, divide boys and girls. Then begin to call out some of the attributes that your students named.

2. After several examples, direct students to return to their seats. Ask students which attributes are the best to use. *(Easily observable, physical attributes generally work best.)*

3. Ask students to name ways to subdivide the larger groups that you divided. Use students' suggestions to make a diagram on the chalkboard similar to the one shown.

4. Point out that scientists use attributes to classify living things. Ask students to name some ways that plants can be grouped. *(By their color, size, or shape of leaves, or by the way they reproduce.)*

5. Pair your students. Give each pair the materials listed on page 7 and one copy of page 9.

6. Instruct the pair to cut apart the cards on the reproducible. Then challenge each pair to use the information on the cards to arrange the cards on the construction paper to make a plant classification chart.

7. Go over the correct arrangement of cards using the answer key on page 95. Instruct each pair to glue the cards in place, connecting the cards with lengths of yarn.

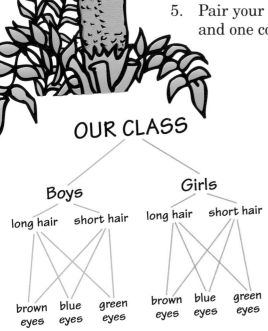

OUR CLASS

Boys   Girls

long hair   short hair   long hair   short hair

brown   blue   green   brown   blue   green
eyes   eyes   eyes   eyes   eyes   eyes

THE PLANT KINGDOM

NONSEED PLANTS WITH ROOTS, STEMS, AND LEAVES

— example: ferns

GYMNOSPERMS

— are seed plants that have cones
— are also called *conifers* or *evergreen trees*
— examples: pine, spruce, fir, cedar, bald cypress, hemlock, redwood, yew, and larch trees

MONOCOTYLEDONS (MONOCOTS)

— are angiosperms that produce seeds having only one *cotyledon,* or seed leaf
— have petals in groups of three
— have leaves with parallel veins
— examples: grasses, palms, lilies, and orchids

SEED PLANTS

— plants that reproduce with seeds

DICOTYLEDONS (DICOTS)

— are angiosperms that produce seeds having two *cotyledons,* or seed leaves
— have petals in groups of four or five
— have leaves with branching veins
— examples: roses, cacti, oak trees, and sunflowers

NONSEED PLANTS

— are plants that do not reproduce with seeds

ANGIOSPERMS

— are seed plants that have flowers
— include all garden and wildflowers, weeds, plants that produce fruits and vegetables, grasses, grains, and all trees and shrubs that lose their leaves in autumn

NONSEED PLANTS WITHOUT ROOTS, STEMS, OR LEAVES

— example: mosses, fungi, and algae

©1998 The Education Center, Inc. • *Lifesaver Lessons*™ • Grade 5 • TEC512 • Key p. 95

How To Extend The Lesson:

• Divide your class into five groups. Assign each group ten different states to research. Have the group find the names and pictures of the state flowers and trees for its assigned states. Challenge the group to use the pictures, what they've learned about plant classification, and reference materials, to identify each state tree as either an *angiosperm* or a *gymnosperm* and each state flower as a *monocot* or a *dicot*. Compile all researched information into a class chart.

• Encourage each student to take a walk through his yard or neighborhood to observe flowering plants. Instruct the student to write careful notes and make detailed drawings of three specimens that he finds. When he returns to school, challenge the student to use these observations and his research skills to find the scientific names of his three plants. Allow each student to share his findings with the class.

• Pair your students and assign the pair two different plant families, such as the rose and the lily. Challenge the pair to create a Venn diagram comparing and contrasting the two plant families. Have students include information on reproduction, growth, physical characteristics, and environment.

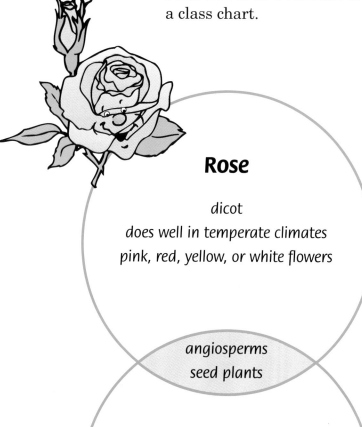

Rose

dicot
does well in temperate climates
pink, red, yellow, or white flowers

angiosperms
seed plants

Lily

monocot
bulb
trumpet-shaped flower with six petals

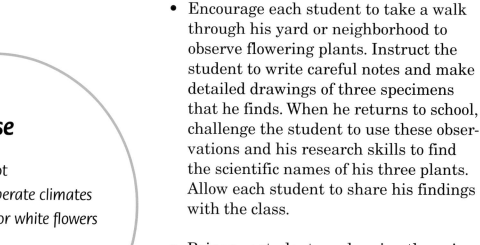

What's Blooming?

*Watch your students' knowledge of flowering plants blossom
with this hands-on lesson.*

Skill: Identifying each part of a flower and its role in reproduction

Estimated Lesson Time: 1 hour

Teacher Preparation:
1. Duplicate one copy of page 13 for each student.
2. Make a transparency of page 13.

Materials:
1 copy of page 13 for each student
1 blank transparency
1 index card for each student
assorted craft materials such as pipe cleaners, yarn, bag ties,
    egg cartons, construction paper, tissue paper, and clay
tape, scissors, and glue

Background Information:
   Flowers are the reproductive parts of *angiosperms* or flowering plants.
A young flower bud is protected by green leaflike parts called
sepals.
   All flowers are made up of the same basic parts that allow a plant to
produce a seed. Most flowers contain both a male part—the *stamen*—
and a female part—the *pistil.* The stamen has an enlarged part called
an *anther* that grows on the end of a long stalk called the *filament.* The
anther produces pollen grains, which develop into sperm. Most pistils
have three main parts: the *stigma, style,* and *ovary.*
   The transfer of pollen from the anther to the stigma is called
pollination. The surface of the stigma is sticky to catch pollen grains. A
pollen grain will swell as it absorbs sugar and water from the stigma,
and it will begin to grow a tube through the slender style down to the
ovary. The ovary contains one or more ovules where egg cells are formed.
Fertilization occurs when a pollen tube enters an ovule in the ovary. The
fertilized egg then develops into a seed and the ovary grows into a structure
called the *fruit.*

Introducing The Lesson:

To begin, have students name the main parts of a green plant—*roots, stem, seeds, leaves, flowers.* Ask students if they know the purpose of a flower. Explain to the class that the flower is the reproductive part of the plant.

Steps:

1. Display the transparency you created of page 13 and distribute one copy of page 13 to each child.

2. Use the Background Information on page 11 to name each flower part and explain its function in the reproduction of a plant. As you discuss each part, write its name on the line next to the appropriate definition. Have each student copy the information from the transparency onto his paper. Then instruct each student to write each numbered word in the appropriate numbered blank of the illustration at the top of page 13. Tell students to use this reproducible as a reference throughout their study of plants.

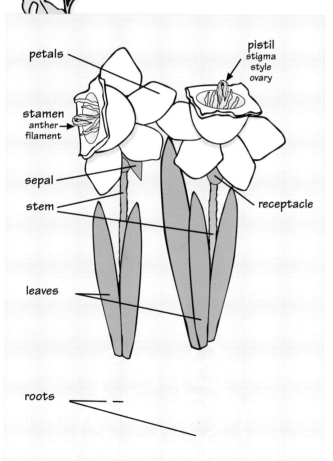

3. Divide the class into groups. Provide each group with scissors, tape, glue, index cards, and a variety of craft materials to choose from.

4. Tell each student to create a model of a flower using any materials that are on his group's table. Instruct him to include on the model all the plant parts that were discussed in this lesson. Have him use page 13 as a reference.

5. Have each student write a paragraph on an index card explaining what he used for each part of the flower. Attach the index card to the model flower and display it in the school media center.

Playing An Important Part

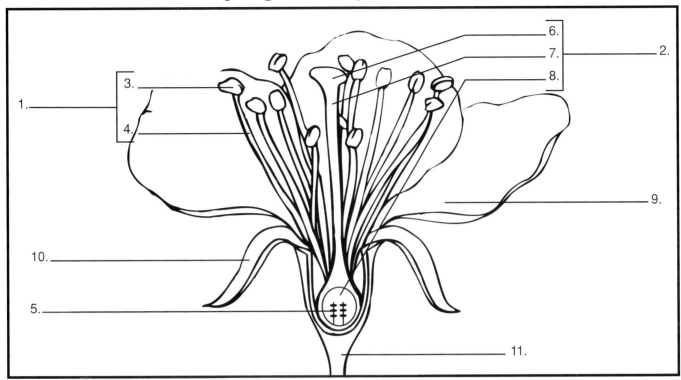

Parts Of A Flower

• anther	• ovules	• pistil	• sepal	• stigma	• ovary
• filament	• petal	• receptacle	• stamen	• style	

Use the diagram above and the clues to help you fill in the correct plant parts.

1. _____ —male reproductive part of a flower

2. _____ —female reproductive part of a flower

3. _____ —produces pollen grains which develop sperm

4. _____ —supports the anther

5. _____ —become the seeds when sperm cells fertilize the egg cells

6. _____ —sticky, pollen-receptive part of the pistil

7. _____ —the stalk of the pistil down which the pollen tube grows

8. _____ —contains the ovules and becomes the fruit

9. _____ —colorful part of a flower used to attract insects and birds

10. _____ —protects the bud of a young flower

11. _____ —reproductive parts of a plant are attached here

Bonus Box: What do you think is the most important part of the flower? Defend your answer on the back of this paper.

13

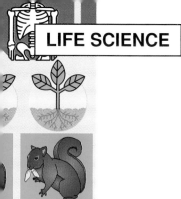

How To Extend The Lesson:

- Discuss the different agents of pollination—insects, birds, and wind. Divide the class into groups. Have each group create a poster using illustrations and labels to show how one of these agents aids in pollination. For example, have students illustrate the following sequence of events:
  1. A bee looks for nectar on a flower.
  2. Pollen collects on its body and legs.
  3. Pollen falls from the bee and sticks to the stigma of a flower.
  4. Pollen grains swell as they absorb sugar and water.
  5. A pollen tube begins to grow through the style.
  6. Fertilization occurs when a pollen tube enters the ovule.
  7. The ovary enlarges and seeds form.

- Have each student write a story about a typical day from the perspective of an insect or a bird that aids in the pollination of flowers.

- Have students research the work of Gregor Mendel and his impact on how plants are grown today. Mendel was a botanist who experimented in crossing plants—taking pollen from one flower and using it to pollinate a flower with an opposite trait.

Spotlight On Cells

Plant and animal cells are center stage with this helpful lesson.

Skill: Identifying the parts of plant and animal cells

Estimated Lesson Time: 1 hour

Teacher Preparation:
1. Copy the diagram from page 16 onto a sheet of chart paper or a transparency.
2. Duplicate a copy of page 17 for each student.
3. Gather the materials listed below.

Materials:
1 sheet of chart paper or a blank transparency
1 copy of page 17 for each student
crayons or colored pencils, scissors, glue, and a 9" x 12" sheet of drawing paper for each student

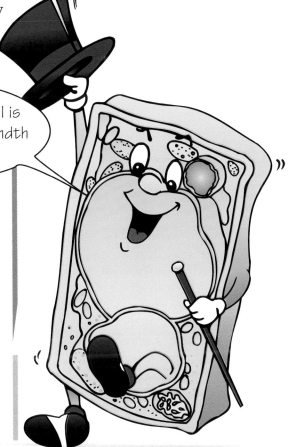

An average animal cell is about one one-thousandth of an inch across.

Background Information:
All living things are made up of one or more cells. A cell is the basic unit of structure and function in an organism. There are billions of life forms that consist of a single cell and can be seen only with a microscope. Larger life forms have millions of cells. These larger organisms not only have a greater number of cells, but also have different kinds of cells within the same body. Each cell's structure and contents allow it to do a specialized job and contribute to the process of keeping the organism alive.

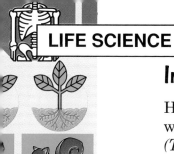
Introducing The Lesson:

Have students name the largest animal they can think of. Then ask them what the tiniest living organism and this large animal have in common. *(They are both composed of cells.)*

Steps:

1. Share the Background Information on page 15 with your students. Point out that cells, like all living things, are made up of parts.

2. Use the diagram and the definitions below to explain the structure and function of each cell part. Explain to students that these are the main parts of a cell, but not all of them.

3. Have students compare the two cells. Help students recognize that plant and animal cells are basically the same, except for two features. Have students identify these features. *(Plant cells have cell walls and chloroplasts; animal cells do not.)*

4. Distribute one copy of page 17, crayons or colored pencils, scissors, glue, and one 9" x 12" sheet of drawing paper to each student. Have the student complete the sheet as directed. Then check and discuss the completed sheets as a class.

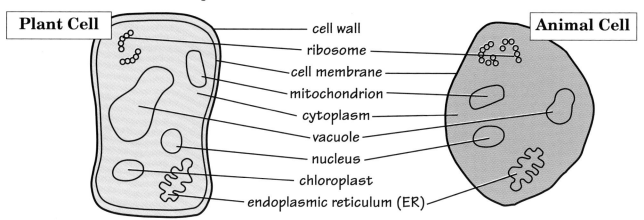

Cell Structures And Their Functions

- **cell wall:** nonliving structure surrounding a **plant** cell; provides shape and support
- **cell membrane:** encloses the cell; controls the inward and outward flow of materials
- **chloroplasts:** contain chlorophyll and are used by **plants** to make food
- **cytoplasm:** jellylike material where chemical processes take place
- **mitochondria:** rodlike structures that release energy from food and supply energy to other parts of the cell
- **vacuoles:** fluid-filled sacs that store different substances in liquid form
- **nucleus:** stores information and controls cell activities; is surrounded by a membrane that separates it from the rest of the cell
- **ribosomes:** particles in cytoplasm that look like small balls; build the proteins needed by a cell
- **endoplasmic reticulum (ER):** a network of membranes that run throughout the cytoplasm and form tubes through which materials move to all cell parts

Name _____

Playing The Perfect Part

Each part of a cell has a special role to play. Color the pictures on the right-hand side of this page. Cut along the dashed lines of each picture at the right. Read each clue; then glue each circle onto the appropriate place of the diagram.

Plant Cell

cell wall
I give a plant cell shape and support.

cell membrane
I control the flow of materials in and out of the cell.

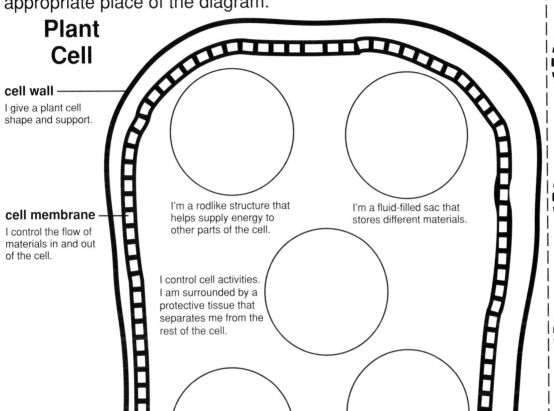

I'm a rodlike structure that helps supply energy to other parts of the cell.

I'm a fluid-filled sac that stores different materials.

I control cell activities. I am surrounded by a protective tissue that separates me from the rest of the cell.

I contain chlorophyll and am used by a plant to make food.

I'm a jellylike material that surrounds the nucleus.

I'm a network of thin tissue that runs throughout the cytoplasm. I help move materials to all cell parts.

I'm a small, ball-like particle in the cytoplasm. I build proteins needed by the cell.

ribosome

nucleus

chloroplast

vacuole

endoplasmic reticulum (ER)

mitochondrion

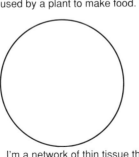

cytoplasm

Note: These are the main parts of a cell, but not all of them. Drawings are not to scale.

Bonus Box: Draw an animal cell on another sheet of paper. Color and label each cell part.

How To Extend The Lesson:

- Review the parts of a plant cell and an animal cell with your students. Then have them suggest various everyday materials that they can associate with each cell part. *(Examples: cell membrane—a mesh bag, chloroplasts—green grapes, ribosomes—candy sprinkles)* Next provide each student with a light-colored, 12" x 18" sheet of construction paper. For homework, direct the student to create a three-dimensional picture of a plant or animal cell using arts-and-crafts supplies and/or odds and ends found around the home. Encourage students to be creative. The following school day, have students share their completed projects. Have them cast their votes for the most creative cells.

A muscle cell

A blood cell

A nerve cell

A fat cell

A skin cell is flat, hard, and tough. It protects the delicate body parts beneath it.

A bone cell

- Follow the directions below to prepare slides of plant and animal cells. Place the slides, a microscope, markers or colored pencils, and a supply of drawing paper at a center. In turn direct each student to the center. Instruct the student to use the microscope (at a high power) to observe the cells. Then have the student draw a labeled picture of what he observed about each cell.

Materials: 2 droppers, 2 slides and coverslips, iodine, toothpick, tweezers, 1 onion

Directions For Preparing Slides:
1. Use a dropper to place a small amount of iodine on a slide. Using the toothpick, gently scrape the inside of your cheek. Place the scraping in the drop of iodine; then cover it with a coverslip.
2. Use a dropper to place a small amount of iodine on a slide. Use the tweezers to peel a thin, clear piece of skin from an inside section of an onion. Place the onion skin in the iodine. Add a coverslip.

- Draw a large outline of a human body and post it on a wall or bulletin board. Place a supply of markers or crayons and reference materials near the board. Remind students that the human body is a complex organism made of different types of cells. (Examples include muscle, blood, nerve, bone, skin, and fat cells.) Pair students and assign each pair a different type of body cell. Direct each pair to use the materials to illustrate a labeled picture of the cell and its parts. In turn have the pair draw its illustration on the body outline and write a caption beside the cell explaining the cell's function.

Spine-Tingling Science

Get "back" to the basics of classification with this exciting lesson!

Skill: Classifying animals as vertebrates and invertebrates

Estimated Lesson Time: 45 minutes

Teacher Preparation:
1. Duplicate the reproducible on page 21 for each student.
2. Collect several pictures of vertebrates and invertebrates from magazines.

Materials:
8–10 pictures of animals (including pictures of both vertebrates and invertebrates)
1 copy of page 21 for each student
2 metal rings for each student

Background Information:
The scientific practice of classifying animals according to similar characteristics is known as *taxonomy*. All living things are divided into a series of groups and subgroups. The largest of these groups is known as a *kingdom*. Scientists classify most living things into two kingdoms—the plant kingdom and the animal kingdom.

The animal kingdom is broken down into subgroups, each of which is called a *phylum*. The phylum *Chordata* is made up of *vertebrates,* animals with backbones. There are about 40,000 species of vertebrates. The major classes of vertebrates include fish, amphibians, reptiles, birds, and mammals.

The remaining phyla are made up of *invertebrates,* animals that do not have backbones. There are more than one million species of invertebrates in the animal kingdom.

Fast Facts:
- Invertebrates make up more than 90 percent of the world's animal population, and vertebrates make up the remaining 10 percent.
- Some invertebrates are microscopic, whereas others, such as the giant squid, are large enough to take on a sperm whale!

Introducing The Lesson:

Explain to students that scientists classify living things into categories based on similar characteristics. Point out that this classification process is known as taxonomy. Have ten student volunteers come to the front of the classroom. Challenge the remaining students to classify the student volunteers into categories based on a physical attribute such as hair color, eye color, or sex. Record the results on the board.

Steps:

1. Continue the classification activity by reclassifying the student volunteers using a different physical attribute. Encourage students to continue to divide each subgroup based on additional similarities and differences.

2. Show your students several pictures of animals that include examples of both vertebrates and invertebrates.

3. Challenge students to group the animal pictures into categories based on their similar characteristics or attributes.

4. On the board record the specific categories students used to classify the animals in the photos.

5. Share the Background Information on page 19 with your students. Explain that one way to classify animals is by determining if they have a backbone. Direct each student to stand and run his fingers up and down the center of his back. Explain that what he feels is his *vertebral column* or backbone.

6. Distribute one copy of page 21 to each student; then have him complete it as directed. Provide each student with two metal rings. Have him use a hole puncher to punch a hole in the upper left-hand corner of each cut-out card from page 21. Direct the student to place the vertebrate cards on one ring and the invertebrate cards on the other ring. Allow students to create other animal cards, placing each card on the appropriate ring.

Doctor, Doctor!

Dr. Kyra Practer has lost her patients' files and needs your help! Dr. Practer sees only patients that have backbones. Help Dr. Practer identify her patients by sorting the following animals using the directions provided.

Directions: Color the cards; then cut them apart. On the back of each card, write the animal's name, its classification (vertebrate or invertebrate), and one interesting fact about the animal.

	clam	turtle	amoeba
	earthworm	**dolphin**	**spider**	**cat**
	rabbit	**jellyfish**	**starfish**	**crab**
	frog	**fish**	**mouse**	**skunk**

How To Extend The Lesson:

• Label a bulletin board with the heading "We've Got Class!" Record each of the five vertebrate classes—fish, amphibians, reptiles, birds, and mammals—on a separate construction-paper strip. Then divide the bulletin board into five sections and staple one of the labeled strips to the top of each section. Challenge students to look through old magazines to find examples of animals that fall into each of the five classes. Staple the animal pictures under the appropriate column to create an eye-catching display.

• Challenge students to learn more about invertebrates with this newsworthy idea! Discuss how an employment advertisement provides information on the credentials needed for a particular job. Divide students into groups; then assign each group one of the invertebrate phyla below. Have each group research information about its phylum and create an employment advertisement that includes the characteristics an organism needs to be successful in that phylum. Have each group share its ad with the rest of the class. Then assemble the ads into a class newspaper titled *Invertebrate Times*.

Protozoans: single-celled microscopic animals
Poriferons: animals with large pores
Coelenterates: water animals with stinging tendons
Ctenophores: animals with rows of little combs covering their bodies
Flatworms: animals that are thin and flat like ribbon
Nematodes: roundworms
Molluscs: soft-bodied animals that have shells to protect themselves
Annelids: segmented worms
Arthropods: animals with jointed legs and segmented bodies
Echinoderms: animals with many spines projecting from their bodies

• Give your students some additional practice with taxonomy by having them classify everyday items into categories based on similar characteristics. Bring in advertisements for automobiles, music CDs, toys, clothing, or any other product that might interest students. Then group students according to their interest in a particular product. Have each group classify the items featured in its advertisement into categories. For example, a group classifying music CDs might have categories for country, rock and roll, rap, and pop music. Direct the group to break down the categories even further based on criteria the group decides to use in its classification process. For example, rock and roll could be further broken down into heavy metal, alternative, and classic rock. Have each group create a chart or diagram to show how it chose to classify the items into categories.

It's All A Balancing Act

Help your students understand the delicate balance between plants, animals, and humans within our environment.

Skill: Recognizing the characteristics of different ecosystems

Estimated Lesson Time: 1 hour

Teacher Preparation:
1. Collect pictures of plants and animals within an ecosystem.
2. Gather research materials on ecosystems.
3. Duplicate one copy of page 25 for each student.

Materials:
pictures of plants and animals from an ecosystem
research materials on ecosystems
6 sheets of chart paper
6 large, light-colored sheets of bulletin-board paper or butcher paper
markers or colored pencils
1 copy of page 25 for each student
encyclopedias

Background Information:
An *ecosystem* includes the community of plants and animals that live within a certain area of our environment. These plants and animals rely on one another for survival: food, shelter, and protection. The earth supports a variety of ecosystems, including *deserts, forests, the tundra, oceans, grasslands,* and *wetlands.* Each ecosystem has its own unique characteristics, such as climate, terrain, and plant and animal life. The connection between the plants and animals within the ecosystem is so strong that any singular change can affect the balance of an entire ecosystem.

Introducing The Lesson:

Show students several pictures of various plants and animals within a particular ecosystem, such as wetlands or a desert. Ask students to explain any relationships between the plants and animals in these pictures. (*Example: The trees are supported by the soil, the coyote lives among trees, the coyote preys upon rabbits, rabbits eat plants, and plants are supported by the soil.*)

Steps:

1. Explain to students that plants, animals, and their surroundings are all linked together. They rely upon one another in what we call an *ecosystem.*

2. Tell students that the earth supports a variety of ecosystems including the following: *deserts, forests, the tundra, oceans, grasslands,* and *wetlands.* Each ecosystem has its own unique characteristics, such as climate, terrain, and plant and animal life. Ask students to name a specific characteristic of one of the ecosystems. (*Examples: The climate of the tundra is very, very cold. Oceans are composed of salt water.*)

3. Divide students into six groups and assign each group an ecosystem. Supply each group with research materials, a large piece of bulletin-board or butcher paper, and markers or colored pencils. Instruct each group to research the climate, terrain, and plant and animal life of its ecosystem. Then have each group draw a mural illustrating the characteristics of its ecosystem. Instruct each group to include at least five examples of interdependence among the inhabitants of its ecosystem. Finally have each group label and color its mural, then share its findings with the rest of the class.

4. Explain to your students that the connection between the plants and animals within an ecosystem is so strong that even a small change can affect the balance of the entire ecosystem. Appoint one member of each group as Recorder, giving each Recorder a piece of chart paper and a marker. Then have the class brainstorm as many changes as possible that would upset the balance of each ecosystem, including interference by humans. As each ecosystem is discussed, have that group's Recorder write the information on his piece of chart paper. Display the murals and the lists of changes in the hallway for all to view.

5. Give one copy of page 25 to each student. Have the student complete the page as directed.

Picture This!

Picture this—you're a world traveler studying the earth's numerous ecosystems: *deserts, forests, the tundra, oceans, grasslands, wetlands*. Each ecosystem has its own characteristics—such as climate, terrain, and plant and animal life—that make it unique.

Directions: Read each sentence below. Decide which ecosystem the sentence is describing. Then write the number of that fact in the appropriate snapshot. If you need help, use an encyclopedia. Bon voyage!

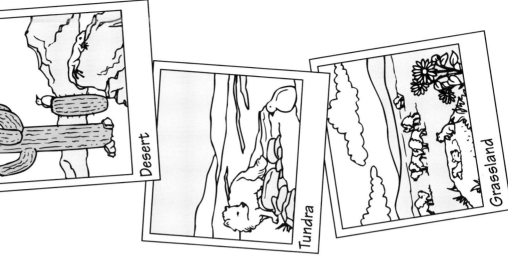

Desert

Tundra

Grassland

1. I'm a large expanse of land covered with tall grasses.
2. I'm also known as a *prairie* or *savanna*.
3. I cover one-seventh of the earth's land surface, but because of environmental changes, that amount is increasing.
4. My temperature range is from less than 0°C to never above 10°C.
5. I cover about 70 percent of the earth's surface.
6. I cover about 30 percent of the earth's land.
7. I receive less than ten inches of moisture a year.
8. I have a variety of plants and animals that live at different depths.
9. Most of my land in the United States has been plowed under and used for agricultural land.
10. I don't receive enough precipitation to support large trees.
11. I provide homes for birds, insects, and animals, as well as sources of medicines.
12. I can be located near an ocean and contain salt water, or in forests and contain freshwater.
13. I'm an area that helps absorb carbon dioxide, produce oxygen, and prevent erosion.
14. I can be located in very cold or very warm climates.
15. The ground below my surface stays frozen all year.
16. I'm the name for the plains of the arctic circle.
17. I'm primarily salt water.
18. Many plants and animals thrive in my hostile environment.
19. I provide homes for birds, fish, animals, and insects.
20. I include many species of fish and invertebrates.
21. My areas contain permanent moisture: bogs, swamps, marshes, estuaries, ponds, lakes, and rivers.
22. I contain tropical, temperate, coniferous, and deciduous trees.

©1998 The Education Center, Inc. • *Lifesaver Lessons*™ • Grade 5 • TEC512 • Key p. 95

Ocean

Wetlands

Forest

How To Extend The Lesson:

- Challenge each student to go to an area in her backyard or a nearby park and to sit quietly for a period of time to observe. Instruct the student to take along a journal or a piece of paper and pencil with which to record her observations. Have the student record as many evidences as possible of interactions among the plants and animals. Have the students bring in their lists on a designated day to share with their classmates.

- Take a field trip to an ecosystem in your area. Instruct students to move through it quietly and to make observations without disturbing the balance of nature. If this is not possible, invite a local expert to your classroom to share photographs and information about a particular ecosystem.

- Have each student write a letter to a national environmental organization expressing his concern and asking how he can get involved in protecting our ecosystems.

- Post a large piece of bulletin-board paper on a wall. Divide this paper into bricklike sections. Then encourage students to find out more about ecosystems of the world by providing books and periodicals with inviting pictures and interesting information. As each student learns something new about an ecosystem, have her write this information in one of the bricks on the wall.

Under The Sea

Take your students on a voyage beneath the waves to explore the four ocean zones with the following research activity.

Skill: Identifying and defining the four ocean zones

Estimated Lesson Time: 1 hour

Teacher Preparation:
1. Make one copy of page 29 for each group.
2. Cut construction paper for each group according to the materials list below.

Materials:
Provide each group with markers, crayons, scissors, and one sheet of construction paper in each of the following colors and dimensions:
- white—12" x 5"
- light blue—12" x 7"
- dark blue—12" x 9"
- black—12" x 11"
- brown—12" x 12"

Background Information:
Descend into the ocean depths, and you will pass through four distinct zones on your way to the ocean floor. The deeper you go, the colder and darker the water becomes.

- The **sunlight zone,** also known as the *epipelagic zone,* is the most productive layer. It lies just beneath the surface of the ocean and extends down to 650 feet. Many plants and animals live in this zone.

- The **twilight zone,** also known as the *mesopelagic zone,* begins at 650 feet and continues down to 3,250 feet. Very little sunlight reaches this zone, so plants cannot grow here. Animals in this zone swim up to the sunlight zone to feed at night.

- The **bathypelagic zone** ends at approximately 19,700 feet below sea level. It is pitch dark in this zone. Very few animals live here. Finding food is very difficult. Some animals eat particles that drift down from the zones above.

- The **hadal zone,** also known as the *abyssopelagic zone,* consists of anything below 19,700 feet, including the ocean floor. Very few animals live here. Finding food is very difficult. Some animals eat particles that drift down from the zones above.

Introducing The Lesson:

Begin the lesson by showing your students a map of the world. Ask your students, "Is there more land or water shown on the map?" After taking several responses, tell your students that water covers 71 percent of the earth's surface.

Steps:

1. Ask your students, "What is the tallest mountain in the world?" *(Mount Everest)* Tell your students that the ocean is very deep and that the deepest trench—the Marianas Trench—is seven miles deep. Tell your students that if you put Mount Everest in this trench, its peak wouldn't even reach the top of the trench.

2. Next tell your students that the ocean is divided into four major zones. Read the Background Information on page 27 to your students to identify the names of the four zones.

3. Divide your students into groups of two or three. Inform each group that it is going to research each ocean zone to find out its location and whether any plants or animals live in it. Tell each group that it will create a flip book to display its findings.

4. Give each group a copy of page 29 and the materials listed on page 27. Instruct the group to carefully follow the directions on page 29 to complete its flip book. Encourage groups to work together and share resources and reference materials.

surface

Mount Everest

one mile deep

seven miles deep

Ocean Zone Flip Book
Research It!

Descend into the ocean depths, and you will pass through four distinct zones on your way to the ocean floor. The deeper you go, the colder and darker the water becomes.

Listed below are the names of the four ocean zones. Research to find out the location of each zone. Also research to find out if any plants or animals live in each zone. Take notes! You will create the flip book described below to display your findings.

- The sunlight zone (epipelagic zone)
- The twilight zone (mesopelagic zone)
- The bathypelagic zone
- The hadal zone (abyssopelagic zone)

Make It!

Materials: markers, crayons, scissors, one sheet of construction paper in each of the following colors and dimensions:
- white—12" x 5"
- light blue—12" x 7"
- dark blue—12" x 9"
- black—12" x 11"
- brown—12" x 12"

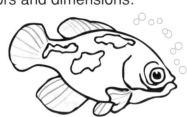

Directions:

Step 1: Carefully trim one 12-inch edge of each sheet of paper (except the brown sheet) in a wavy pattern as shown. No more than one-half inch should be trimmed off. This will form the bottom edge of the page.

Step 2: Stack the colored paper in the following order: white (top sheet), light blue, dark blue, black, and brown (bottom sheet). Be sure that the bottom edge of each sheet is visible as shown.

Step 3: Staple all the sheets together at the top to bind the booklet.

Step 4: The brown, black, dark blue, and light blue pages represent the four zones of the ocean. Label the bottom of each page with the appropriate zone name. On each page, include drawings of plant and animal life found in that zone as well as a brief description of the zone.

Step 5: Decorate the white cover with illustrations and the title "Under The Sea."

Step 1:

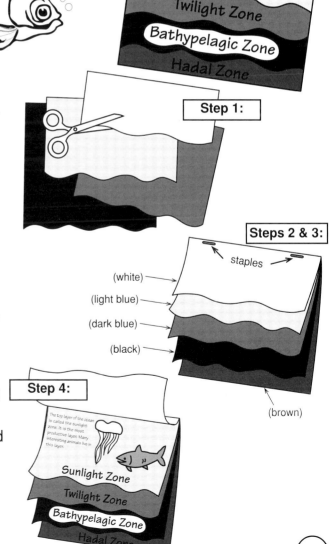

Steps 2 & 3:
staples
(white)
(light blue)
(dark blue)
(black)
(brown)

Step 4:
Sunlight Zone
Twilight Zone
Bathypelagic Zone
Hadal Zone

How To Extend The Lesson:

- There are many strange and interesting facts about what lurks beneath the surface of the ocean. Have your students research some of these interesting and strange facts. Display their findings on a bulletin board similar to the example below.

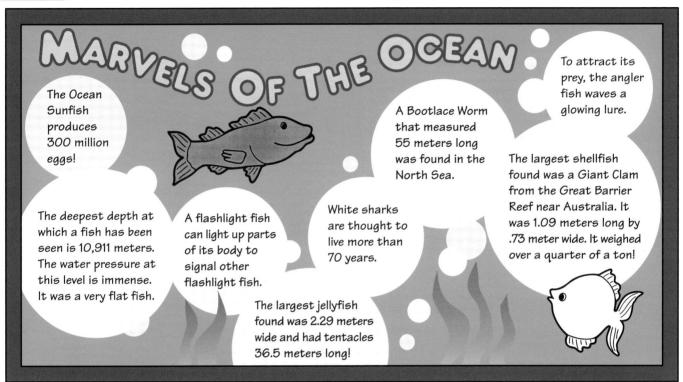

- Survival is a daily challenge for creatures of the sea. Many sea animals have developed special characteristics that help protect them from predators. Have your students research the various ways sea creatures protect themselves, such as *camouflage, countershading, disruptive coloration,* and *false eye spots.* Have each student illustrate the animal he researches and write a brief paragraph explaining his creature's unique feature(s). Compile the illustrations and paragraphs into a book for your students to enjoy during your study of the ocean.

Go With The Flow

Expose your students to the wonders of the human circulatory system with this hands-on lesson.

Skill: Recognizing and identifying the components of the circulatory system

Estimated Lesson Time: 45 minutes

Teacher Preparation:
1. Make a copy of page 33 for each group of students.
2. Cut one 5-foot sheet of white bulletin-board paper for each group of students.

Materials:
1 empty one-quart milk or juice container
1 bucket (5 quarts or larger)
1 copy of page 33 for each group of students
blue and red yarn
one 5-foot sheet of white bulletin-board or butcher paper for each group of students
scissors and glue for each group of students

Background Information:
The circulatory system transports food and oxygen all over the body. The heart acts as a pump for the blood, which flows through a complex series of *arteries, capillaries,* and *veins.* The blood flowing through the arteries carries oxygenated blood and dissolved food. The arteries divide into smaller blood vessels called capillaries. Oxygen and food pass through the capillary walls into the cells of the body. Blood leaving the capillaries has lost its oxygen and carries waste products away from the body's cells. The capillaries join together to form larger vessels called veins. Veins carry deoxygenated blood and waste products back to the heart. The used blood then goes to the lungs, where it expels carbon dioxide and is refreshed with oxygen. It takes blood about one minute to make a complete circuit around the body.

The circulatory system 31

Introducing The Lesson:

Show your students a one-quart carton. Explain that an average person's body contains nearly five quarts of blood, or five one-quart cartons. Demonstrate how much blood that is by filling up the carton with water and dumping it into a bucket five times.

Steps:

1. Ask students to volunteer information they know about how blood circulates through the body. Record students' responses on the board.

2. Share with your students the Background Information on page 31.

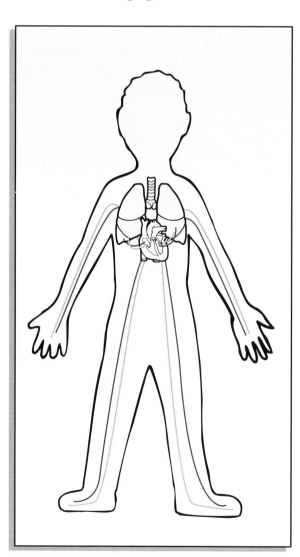

3. Remind students that this process takes place in a short amount of time and that the heart is a very strong muscle.

4. Divide your students into groups of four. Provide each group with a copy of page 33 and a five-foot piece of chart paper, blue and red yarn, scissors, and glue.

5. Direct each group to complete page 33 as directed to create a model of the human circulatory system.

6. Display the completed models in the hall for others to view.

Go With The Flow

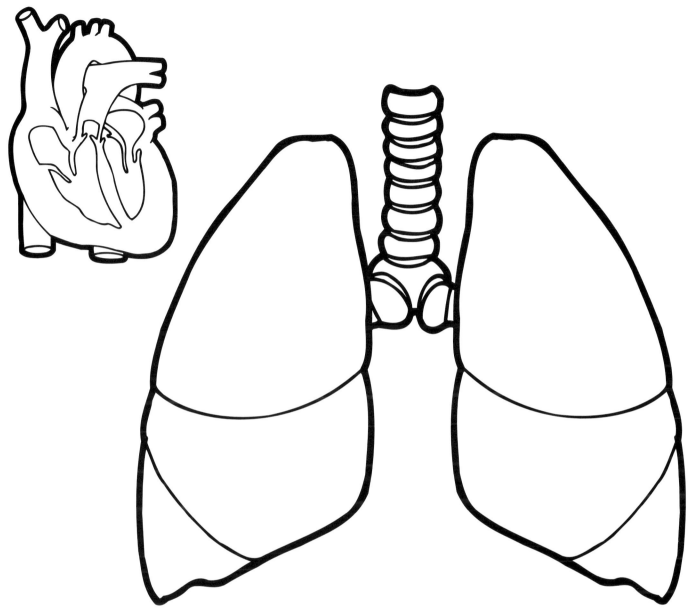

Directions for mapping the flow of blood in the human body:

1. Lay the paper provided by your teacher on the floor. Have one group member lie on the paper faceup. Use a pencil to carefully trace an outline of the student's body.
2. Cut out the heart and lungs on this sheet.
3. Glue the organs in the correct location on your group's paper outline.
4. Glue lengths of red yard, representing oxygenated blood, from the heart down to each hand and each foot.
5. Glue lengths of blue yarn, representing deoxygenated blood, going from each hand and foot back to the heart.
6. Glue additional lengths of blue yarn from the heart to the lungs to show the flow of blood as it moves to the lungs to be reoxygenated.
7. Finally, attach more red yarn from the lungs back to the heart to show the flow of reoxygenated blood from the lungs to the heart.
8. Have each group member sign his or her name at the bottom of your life-size diagram.

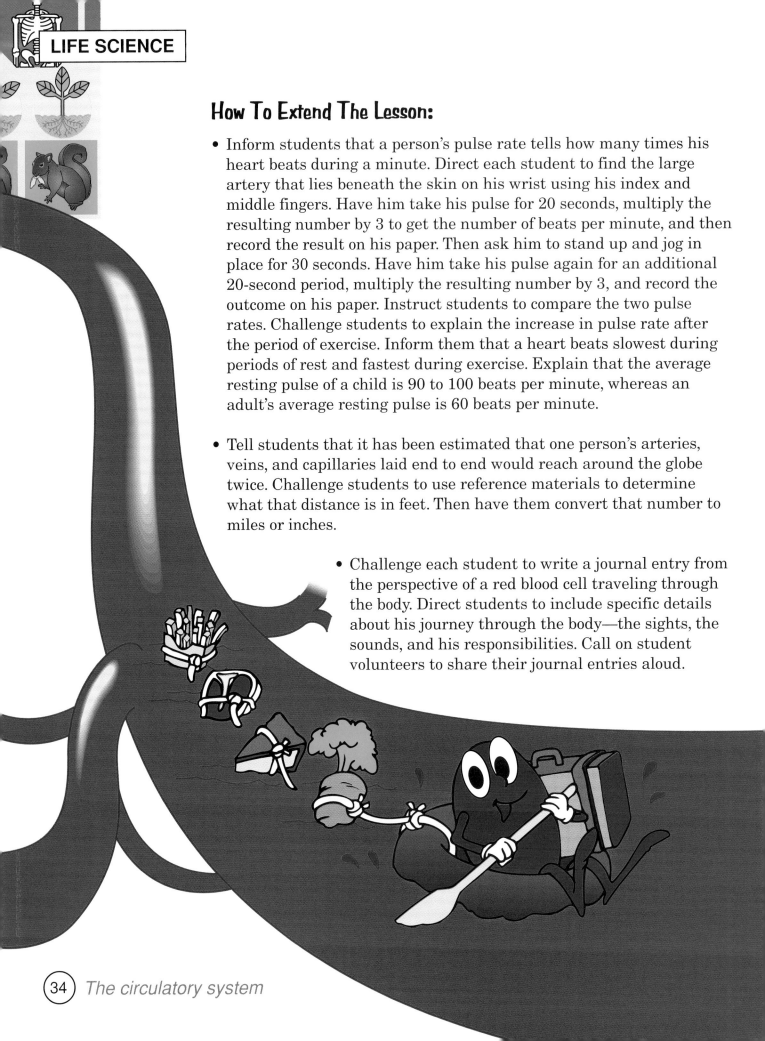

How To Extend The Lesson:

- Inform students that a person's pulse rate tells how many times his heart beats during a minute. Direct each student to find the large artery that lies beneath the skin on his wrist using his index and middle fingers. Have him take his pulse for 20 seconds, multiply the resulting number by 3 to get the number of beats per minute, and then record the result on his paper. Then ask him to stand up and jog in place for 30 seconds. Have him take his pulse again for an additional 20-second period, multiply the resulting number by 3, and record the outcome on his paper. Instruct students to compare the two pulse rates. Challenge students to explain the increase in pulse rate after the period of exercise. Inform them that a heart beats slowest during periods of rest and fastest during exercise. Explain that the average resting pulse of a child is 90 to 100 beats per minute, whereas an adult's average resting pulse is 60 beats per minute.

- Tell students that it has been estimated that one person's arteries, veins, and capillaries laid end to end would reach around the globe twice. Challenge students to use reference materials to determine what that distance is in feet. Then have them convert that number to miles or inches.

- Challenge each student to write a journal entry from the perspective of a red blood cell traveling through the body. Direct students to include specific details about his journey through the body—the sights, the sounds, and his responsibilities. Call on student volunteers to share their journal entries aloud.

Lights, Camera, Digestion!

Use this lesson to introduce your students to the star-studded cast responsible for human digestion.

Skills: Identifying the parts and function of the digestive system

Estimated Lesson Time: 45 minutes

Teacher Preparation:
1. Duplicate one copy of page 37 for each student.
2. Cut three lengths of yarn.

Materials:
1 copy of page 37 for each student
3 lengths of yarn cut to 1 foot, 3 feet, and 30 feet
scissors
glue

Background Information:
The digestive system is made up of a group of organs that break food down for use in the body. The broken-down food particles that result from the process of digestion provide the body with necessary nutrients.

The main part of the digestive system is the alimentary canal, a tube that begins at the mouth and continues on through the pharynx, esophagus, stomach, small intestine, large intestine, and rectum. An average human's alimentary canal is about 30 feet long.

Fast Facts:
- The human mouth makes about 1/2 quart of saliva a day. The body secretes more than 7 quarts of digestive juices daily.

- The appendix is a remnant of a longer intestine. Animals that graze for their food use the appendix for fermentation.

- The average person eats about 3 pounds of food each day or 1,095 pounds of food each year.

Identifying the parts of the digestive system (35)

WOW! That's long!

Introducing The Lesson:

Have three student volunteers come to the front of the classroom. Give each volunteer a precut length of yarn and have him display it for the rest of the class. Challenge the remaining students to guess which length of yarn represents the length of the *alimentary canal,* the series of connected digestive organs that begins at the mouth and extends to the rectum.

Steps:

1. Have each student record his guess—1 foot, 3 feet, or 30 feet—on a scrap of paper.

2. Call on several student volunteers to share their answers and the reasons for the choices they make.

3. Explain that the answer is 30 feet. Tell your students that the human digestive system is made up of about 30 feet of connected organs known as the *alimentary canal.* Point out that the alimentary canal includes the mouth, pharynx, esophagus, stomach, small intestine, large intestine, and rectum.

4. Ask your students to explain how it is possible for 30 feet of organs to fit inside a human body. Guide the students into understanding that many of the organs must bend in order to fit into the body cavity. Coil up the yarn to demonstrate that point.

5. Explain to the class that when a person eats, he first places food in his *mouth.* Then the *pharynx* pushes the chewed food into the *esophagus.* The esophagus then moves in wavelike contractions and pushes the food into the *stomach.*

6. Share with students that special juices in the stomach help digest the food. Tell students that the resulting mixture is then emptied into the *small intestine,* where juices from the *pancreas, liver,* and the intestinal wall continue to digest the food. Point out that the remaining undigested food is then passed into the *large intestine* and then out of the body through the *rectum.*

7. To further investigate the digestive system, provide each student with scissors, glue, and a copy of page 37. Have him complete the activity as directed.

Meet The Cast

As food travels along the path to complete digestion, it comes into contact with a diverse cast of characters (organs), each of whom plays an important part in completing digestion.

Directions: Cut out each filmstrip square. Read the information on each square; then decide the order in which food meets the cast of characters as it flows through the digestive system. Glue the strips in order by placing each strip on the bottom of the one before it.

►► Cast Of Characters

The Small Intestine	The Esophagus
The Pharynx	The Mouth
The Large Intestine	The Stomach

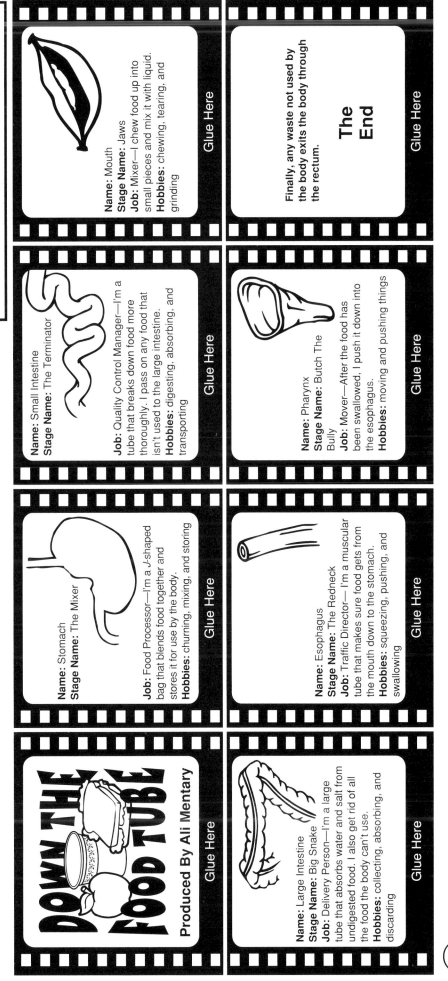

Name: Mouth
Stage Name: Jaws
Job: Mixer—I chew food up into small pieces and mix it with liquid.
Hobbies: chewing, tearing, and grinding

Glue Here

Finally, any waste not used by the body exits the body through the rectum.

The End

Glue Here

Name: Small Intestine
Stage Name: The Terminator

Job: Quality Control Manager—I'm a tube that breaks down food more thoroughly. I pass on any food that isn't used to the large intestine.
Hobbies: digesting, absorbing, and transporting

Glue Here

Name: Pharynx
Stage Name: Butch The Bully
Job: Mover—After the food has been swallowed, I push it down into the esophagus.
Hobbies: moving and pushing things

Glue Here

Name: Stomach
Stage Name: The Mixer

Job: Food Processor—I'm a *J*-shaped bag that blends food together and stores it for use by the body.
Hobbies: churning, mixing, and storing

Glue Here

Name: Esophagus
Stage Name: The Redneck
Job: Traffic Director— I'm a muscular tube that makes sure food gets from the mouth down to the stomach.
Hobbies: squeezing, pushing, and swallowing

Glue Here

DOWN THE FOOD TUBE

Produced By Ali Mentary

Glue Here

Name: Large Intestine
Stage Name: Big Snake
Job: Delivery Person—I'm a large tube that absorbs water and salt from undigested food. I also get rid of all the food the body can't use.
Hobbies: collecting, absorbing, and discarding

Glue Here

©1998 The Education Center, Inc. • *Lifesaver Lessons*™ • Grade 5 • TEC512 • Key p. 95

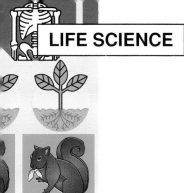

How To Extend The Lesson:

• Divide your students into groups of three or four. Give each group a large sheet of chart paper. Have each group trace the outline of one of its members onto the chart paper. Then direct the students to use construction paper, scissors, and glue to make a model of the digestive system for the outline. Post the completed outlines in your classroom and refer to them throughout your study of the digestive system.

Yum! This tastes sweet!

• Remind students that digestion begins in the mouth. Explain to students that saliva excreted in the mouth contains enzymes that help break food down. Point out that one of these enzymes, *amylase,* turns starches into sugars during the digestive process. Demonstrate the process of turning starches into sugars by giving each student a saltine cracker. Have the student bite the cracker and hold it in his mouth for several minutes before swallowing it. Then have the student describe how the cracker's taste changed. *(The starch in the cracker turns to sugar, and the cracker tastes sweet.)*

• Challenge each student to assume the identity of his favorite food. Have the student write a narrative as if he were the food being consumed by a fifth-grade student during lunch. Encourage the student to include specific details about the trip he takes through the fifth grader's digestive system. Have each student share his completed narrative with the rest of the class. Post the narratives on a bulletin board titled "Adventures In Digestion."

Get The Facts!

Help students investigate the effects of drugs on the human body with this thought-provoking lesson.

Skill: Identifying the effects of chemical substances (drugs) on the human body

Estimated Lesson Time: 1 hour

Teacher Preparation:
1. Copy the Background Information on this page onto a transparency or the chalkboard.
2. Duplicate one copy of page 41 for each student.
3. Label each of three sheets of chart paper with one of these letters: *K, W,* and *L.*

Materials:
1 copy of page 41 for each student
3 sheets of large chart paper
reference materials, such as encyclopedias, library books, etc.
1 blank transparency (optional)
1 marker

Background Information:
Any substance that affects the way a person's mind or body works is a *drug.* Using a drug in a way that disrupts a healthy and productive lifestyle is called *drug abuse.* Drug abuse can take place at any level in society, affecting the rich, the poor, the young, and the old. Any type of drug—including alcohol, nicotine, and prescription medications—can be abused. There are several different types of drugs.
- *stimulants*—drugs that speed up the activity of the nervous system. Examples of stimulants include caffeine, cocaine, nicotine, and synthetic drugs known as *amphetamines.*
- *depressants* (also called *antianxiety and hypnotic drugs*)—reduce tension and worry by slowing down the nervous system. Some examples of depressants include tranquilizers, sedatives, and alcohol.
- *hallucinogens*— drugs that alter what a person sees, feels, or hears. LSD, marijuana, mescaline, and PCP are some examples of hallucinogenic drugs.
- *inhalants*—chemicals that are sniffed to create a high. An inhalant can be one of about 2,000 dangerous chemicals, such as glue, gasoline, nail polish, and aerosol sprays.

The abuse of drugs can have very harmful effects on the human body, such as liver and brain damage, a heart attack, a stroke, and the contraction of AIDS.

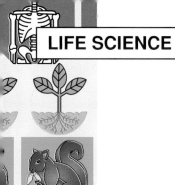

Introducing The Lesson:

Use the three labeled sheets of chart paper to construct a K-W-L chart. Ask students to tell you what they *know* about drugs and the effects of drugs on the human body. List their responses on the first sheet of chart paper labeled *K*. Next ask students what they *want to know* about drugs. Do not answer their questions, but record them on the second sheet of chart paper labeled *W*.

Steps:

1. Explain that a *drug* can be any substance that affects the brain or body.

2. Have students brainstorm a list of substances that they would classify as drugs. Then ask students, "Can a drug be good for one person, yet bad for another?" Elicit the responses that not all drugs are bad, but all drugs can be abused.

3. Share with students the Background Information on page 39.

4. Divide your class into four groups. Assign each group one of the four types of drugs listed on page 39. Encourage each group to use reference materials to research its topic. Have the group prepare a pamphlet, poster, or skit giving information about the type of drug it researched and the effects this type of drug has on the human body. Then have each group make its presentation to the rest of the class.

5. Provide each student with one copy of page 41 to complete as directed.

6. Point out the third chart labeled *L*. Throughout your study on drugs, continue to complete this chart by listing what students have *learned* about drugs and their effects on the human body. Also answer any questions from the *W* chart that may not have been addressed in this unit.

K What We Know:	W What We Want To Know:	L What We've Learned:

Name _____

Getting The Facts Straight

Before you can make a wise decision, it's important to get all the facts! Think about what you've learned about drugs and alcohol and the effects they have on your mind and body. Then read each statement below, and decide if it is true or false. Color the magnifying glass that shows your decision.

	true	false
1. Students who use marijuana find it hard to remember what they've learned.	A	J
2. Wine is safer than beer or liquor.	C	O
3. Adults will not get addicted to alcohol since it is legal for them to drink.	D	H
4. A wine cooler is just the same as fruit punch.	P	I
5. Abusing drugs could lead to a life spent in jail.	E	Z
6. Some kids experiment with drugs because their friends use drugs.	S	J
7. Abusing an inhalant can cause death, even on the first try.	M	V
8. Using drugs could lead to death.	N	X
9. It is okay for someone to drive if he has only had two or three alcoholic drinks.	F	Y
10. Children's bodies can handle the effects of alcohol better than adults'.	L	W
11. Only people from poor communities can get addicted to cocaine.	U	R
12. It is okay to refuse to ride with someone who is drunk.	T	Q
13. People who use drugs can harm the lives of others.	G	K

Solve the mysterious message below by writing the letter that you colored for each matching number shown below.

6 1 9 4 8 13 : 8 2 12 3 5 : 6 7 1 11 12 : 10 1 9 12 2 13 2 !

How To Extend The Lesson:

- Encourage students to seek accurate information to answer their questions regarding drugs and drug abuse. Place a box on your desk in which students can deposit written questions they have about drugs, alcohol, or personal problems related to drug abuse. Answer the questions of a nonpersonal nature during a specified class time. Respond privately to more personal questions by meeting with the child one-on-one. For a serious problem, seek the help of your school nurse or guidance counselor, community drug hot line, or other area resources.

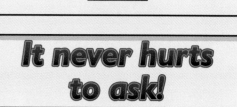

It never hurts to ask!

- Help students learn the skills of wise decision making with this idea. Write each of the following situations on several index cards. Pair students and provide each pair with a card. Direct the pair to read the card, then discuss how it would handle the situation. Next have each pair role-play its situation and solution.

> You're visiting a friend. His parents have gone to the store. He takes a beer from the refrigerator, begins to drink it, and asks you to have one too. What do you do?

> One of your friends is having a lot of problems at home. Lately he is getting behind in school and seems to be avoiding his good friends. You suspect that he is using drugs to "help" with his problems. What do you do?

> You've just found out that your older sister has been to a party where some people were doing drugs. You think she tried the drugs, and you want to talk to her about it. What do you say?

> You've finally been invited to a party given by the "coolest" kids in school. But now you hear that there will be alcohol and drugs at the party. You really want these kids to like you, but you don't want to mess around with drugs and alcohol. What do you do?

> You really want to be friends with a certain cool group of kids at school. Finally one of the cool kids walks up to you and asks you to go to the mall with him. He slips a package of marijuana in your hand and says all you have to do is show up with it. What do you do?

42 *Identifying the effects of drugs on the human body*

Presto Change-O!

Show your students the magic of matter with the following lesson on physical and chemical changes!

Skill: Identifying physical and chemical changes in matter

Estimated Lesson Time: 45 minutes

Teacher Preparation:
1. Make one copy of page 45 for each student.
2. Make an overhead transparency of the chart at the right (or copy the information onto a sheet of chart paper).

Materials:
1 blank transparency and a transparency pen or 1 sheet of chart paper and a marker
1 20-ounce plastic soda bottle
1/2 cup vinegar
2 tablespoons baking soda
1 medium-sized balloon
tape
1 cookie
knife
1 copy of page 45 for each student

	Definite Shape?	Definite Size?	Examples
Solid	yes	yes	wood iron glass
Liquid	no	yes	water gasoline milk
Gas	no	no	air oxygen carbon dioxide

Background Information:

Everything in the universe is made up of *matter*. Matter comes in three different states: *solid, liquid,* and *gas*. The chart above shows characteristics and examples of each state of matter.

There are two kinds of changes that occur in the matter around us all the time: *physical changes* and *chemical changes*. However, these two kinds of changes are very different from each other. A physical change takes place when only the physical characteristics of a substance are changed, and it is still the same substance. For example, wood is chopped, glass is broken, or ice is melted. Changing its state, such as from a solid to a liquid or a liquid to a gas, is also a physical change in matter. When a substance undergoes a physical change, it can usually be changed back to its original size, shape, or appearance. A chemical change takes place when the properties of one substance are changed so that a new substance with different properties is formed. Some examples of chemical changes are the burning of wood, the rusting of iron, or the digestion of food. For a chemical change to occur, energy is either needed or given off during the process.

Introducing The Lesson:

Ask student volunteers to look around the room and give examples of matter—such as a chair, the chalkboard, the water fountain, and air. Next have each student volunteer tell what state of matter *(solid, liquid, or gas)* the thing is that he has named. Display the transparency or chart-paper drawing that you created of the chart on page 43. Briefly review the three states of matter and the characteristics and examples of each.

Steps:

1. Share with students the second paragraph in the Background Information on page 43.

2. Complete the teacher demonstration below for your students. Then ask students the following questions:
   - What two substances did I begin with? *(baking soda and vinegar)*
   - What happened when the two substances were mixed together? *(They bubbled. Then the balloon inflated.)*
   - What type of change occurred? *(a chemical change)*
   - Why? *(A new substance, carbon dioxide gas, was formed when the two original substances were mixed together.)*

Teacher Demonstration

Materials: 1 20-ounce plastic soda bottle, 1/2 cup vinegar, 2 tablespoons baking soda, 1 medium-sized balloon, tape

Directions:
1. Pour the vinegar into the soda bottle.
2. Have a student volunteer hold the mouth of the balloon open as wide as possible. Then carefully place the baking soda inside the balloon.
3. Without allowing any of the baking soda to escape into the bottle, place the mouth of the balloon over the mouth of the bottle. Use the tape to secure the balloon to the bottle.
4. Raise the balloon slowly to allow the baking soda to empty into the bottle.

3. Use a knife to cut a cookie into four pieces. Then ask students the following questions:
   - What substance did I begin with? *(a cookie)*
   - What happened to the substance when it was cut with the knife? *(It was divided into four separate pieces.)*
   - What type of change occurred? *(a physical change)*
   - Why? *(Only the shape and size of the cookie changed. No new substance was formed. It is still a cookie.)*

4. Distribute one copy of page 45 to each student. Instruct students to complete the reproducible as directed. After each student completes the activity, discuss the answers as a class.

Presto Change-O!

Each top hat contains a picture of a change in matter and a description of the picture. Wave your magic wand and decide whether the change is physical or chemical. Then write your answer on the line at the top of each hat.

1. _____

breaking a pencil lead

2. _____

tarnishing of silver

3. _____

digesting food

4. _____

melting of an ice cube

5. _____

crumpling a piece of paper

6. _____

slicing a loaf of bread

7. _____

burning a match

8. _____

making lemonade

9. _____

rusting of a nail

Bonus Box: On the back of this paper, draw three more examples of changes in matter, including both physical and chemical changes. Then label each.

45

How To Extend The Lesson:

- Provide your students with a better understanding of physical and chemical change by gathering a variety of the items mentioned on page 45. Then conduct a teacher demonstration or set up stations for students to observe firsthand the chemical and physical changes taking place.

- Give each student a sheet of drawing paper and crayons, markers, or colored pencils. Instruct her to illustrate an indoor or outdoor scene that shows several examples of physical and chemical changes. For example, she might draw the inside of her kitchen with physical changes taking place, such as water being boiled, bread being sliced, or spaghetti being cooked. Also, she might illustrate chemical changes, such as a pie being baked in the oven or an egg being scrambled on the stove. Direct the student to label each scene in her picture as a physical change or a chemical change; then have her color her picture.

- Supply each student with one 12" x 18" sheet of construction paper, scissors, and glue. Instruct him to divide the paper into two equal sections and then label the sections "Chemical Change" and "Physical Change." Next direct the student to search through magazines and newspapers for pictures that represent each kind of change. Have him cut out each picture and glue it to the appropriate section.

Feeling Hot, Hot, Hot!

Familiarize your students with the hot topics of conduction, convection, and radiation.

Skill: Identifying heat, temperature, conduction, convection, and radiation

Estimated Lesson Time: 45 minutes

Teacher Preparation:
Make one copy of page 49 for each student.

Materials:
1 copy of page 49 for each student
1 large, flat rubber band for each student
1 candle
3 or 4 wooden matches

Background Information:
- *Heat* is a form of energy that a substance has because of the motion of its molecules. The more heat a substance gains, the faster its molecules move. If a substance loses heat, its molecules will move slower.
- *Temperature* is a measure of how hot or cold something is. It is measured in degrees.
- Heat flows in three ways: *conduction, convection,* and *radiation*.
- *Conduction* is heat moving through a solid object. Example: heat traveling through the bottom of a cooking pot.
- *Convection* is the transfer of heat by a moving gas or liquid.
  Example: heat from a hair dryer.
- *Radiation* is heat moving through space as energy waves.
  Example: heat from the sun.

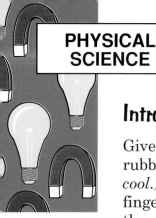

Introducing The Lesson:

Give each student one large, flat rubber band. Instruct the student to touch the rubber band to his forehead. Ask students how the rubber band feels. *(It should feel cool.)* Direct each student to stretch a small portion of the rubber band between two fingers as shown below and then touch it to his forehead again. Ask students how the rubber band feels now. *(The rubber band should feel warmer.)*

Steps:

1. Explain to students that they have just produced a little bit of *heat*. Share the definition of heat from the Background Information on page 47. Ask your students what they think will happen if they repeat the process above several times. Accept all student responses; then have each student try it. *(Each time the rubber band is stretched, it will produce heat and feel warmer.)*

2. Collect the rubber bands. Then tell your students that there are three ways heat can travel: *conduction, convection,* and *radiation.* Use the Background Information to define each method. Point out that heat can move only from a hotter area to one that has a lower temperature. Explain that the heat of the rubber band being transferred to skin is an example of conduction.

3. Demonstrate convection by first lighting a candle. Hold an unlit match next to the base of the flame and observe what happens. *(The match will not ignite.)* Next hold the match above the flame and observe what happens. *(The match will ignite.)* Ask students to explain what has happened. *(Heat rises, so the match can be lit from above the flame; however, if the match is held close to the bottom of the flame, it will not light.)* Repeat with the other matches held at varying heights above the flame.

4. Explain that the best example of radiation is the sun. The air above the earth is not warmed by the sun, but the earth's surface is.

5. Distribute one copy of page 49 to each student. Instruct students to complete the reproducible as directed.

Off To Some Place Cooler!

Did you know that heat travels only from a hotter area to one that is cooler? And there are only three ways that it can get there: conduction, convection, and radiation. *Conduction* is heat moving through a solid object. *Convection* is the transfer of heat by a moving gas or liquid. *Radiation* is heat moving through space as energy waves.

Identify each picture below as an example of conduction, convection, or radiation. Write your answers on the lines provided.

1. _____

2. _____

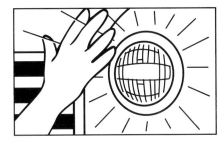

3. _____

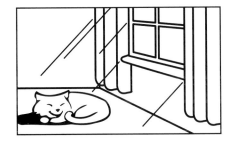

4. _____

5. _____

6. _____

7. _____

8. _____

9. _____

10. _____

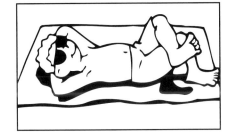

11. _____

12. _____

Bonus Box: On the back of this page, write examples of conduction, convection, and radiation that were not shown above.

49

©1998 The Education Center, Inc. • *Lifesaver Lessons*™ • Grade 5 • TEC512 • Key p. 96

How To Extend The Lesson:

- Reinforce the concept of *conduction* with this hands-on project. Divide your students into groups of three or four. Tell each group that on the following day it will receive a tin can and an ice cube. Explain to each group that its mission is to design a container using materials from home and from school that will keep the ice cube from melting as long as possible. Instruct each student to bring any materials for his container to school the next day. Tell students that there are only three rules: no ice buckets, coolers, or ice may be used for the container; the tin can must be used in some way; and the ice cube must be accessible for periodic checks.

  On the next school day, give each group time to construct its container. Provide additional materials such as plastic bags, tape, Styrofoam® pieces, empty cartons or boxes, tinfoil, and pieces of wood or plastic for each group to use. Once each container has been built, give each group an ice cube to place in its container. Place all the containers in the same area of the classroom. Plan for each group to check its cube once every hour (when the cubes become small, have them checked more frequently). Declare the team whose cube lasts the longest—the team that has reduced conduction the most—the winner.

HOT   TEPID   COLD

- Use this activity to demonstrate that a person's sense of hot and cold is not reliable. Fill three bowls with water, each with a different temperature—hot, tepid, and cold. Invite student volunteers one at a time to dip one hand in the cold water and the other in the hot water for one minute. Then have the student place both hands in the tepid water. Have the student describe how his hands feel. *(The water will feel warm to the hand that was in the cold water, but it will feel cold to the hand that was in the hot water.)* Have students discuss possible explanations for this outcome.

Consider The Source

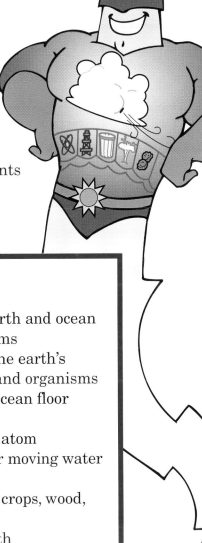

Familiarize students with the sources of energy available today.

Skill: Identifying the main sources of energy used today

Estimated Time Needed: 45 minutes

Teacher Preparation:
Duplicate one copy of page 53 for each of nine
groups of students.

Materials:
1 copy of page 53 for each of nine groups of students
encyclopedias or other reference materials
chalk

Background Information:
There are nine sources of energy as follows:
- *natural gas*—a fossil fuel pumped from wells under the earth and ocean floor formed from fossilized remains of plants and organisms
- *coal*—a fossil fuel mined underground or from beds near the earth's surface that are formed from fossilized remains of plants and organisms
- *oil*—a fossil fuel pumped from wells under the earth and ocean floor formed from fossilized remains of plants and organisms
- *nuclear energy*—the energy locked up in the nucleus of an atom
- *hydropower* (water power)—energy produced from falling or moving water
- *solar energy*—energy from the sun
- *biomass*—energy from plants and organic matter (such as crops, wood, manure, garbage, or sewage)
- *geothermal energy*—heat energy from deep within the earth
- *wind energy*—using the power of the wind for energy

A *renewable energy source* is one that is easily replaced. A *nonrenewable energy source* is one that is used up faster than it can be replaced in a person's lifetime.

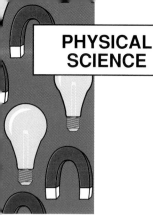
Introducing The Lesson:

Write the sentence below on the chalkboard. Then have each student fill in the blank.

Energy is important in my life because _____.

Steps:

1. Guide students to realize that energy is used for playing sports, cooking, heating and cooling homes, and countless other activities.

2. Explain that scientists are faced with the challenge of finding safe and inexpensive ways to supply the world with energy.

3. Name and briefly describe the nine sources of energy *(coal, oil, natural gas, nuclear, hydropower, solar, geothermal, biomass, and wind)* listed in the Background Information on page 51.

4. Ask students when they have used some of these sources of energy before. *(solar energy for a calculator, wind energy for sailing, petroleum for cars, and electricity)*

5. Divide your class into nine groups, assigning each group a different energy source. Provide each group with one copy of page 53 and access to encyclopedias or other reference materials.

6. Instruct each group to research its assigned energy source to find out what it is, how it works, whether it's renewable or nonrenewable, its advantages and disadvantages, and what this source of energy is currently used for. Have the group record this information on page 53.

7. Afterwards, allow each group to share its information with the class.

Did you know?
The first hydroelectric dam was constructed at Niagara Falls, NY, in the late 1800s.

It takes hundreds of millions of years for fossil-fuel deposits to form.

During World War II, gas from decomposing chicken manure was used as an automobile fuel.

Transportation consumes 63% of the total oil used in the United States.

Consider The Source!

_____
source

What is it? _____

_____

_____

How does it work? _____

_____

_____

This source of energy is: RENEWABLE ☐   NONRENEWABLE ☐

Advantages	Disadvantages

This source of energy is currently used for _____

_____

_____

©1998 The Education Center, Inc. • *Lifesaver Lessons*™ • Grade 5 • TEC512

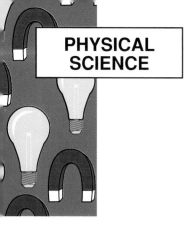

How To Extend The Lesson:

- As a class, brainstorm the different ways that individuals can conserve energy. Give each student a 5" x 12" sheet of tagboard and a same-sized sheet of newsprint. On the newsprint, have each student design a bumper sticker in pencil that promotes energy conservation. When he is satisfied with his design, have the student copy it onto the tagboard and color it with crayons or markers. Post the completed bumper stickers on a bulletin board titled "Honk For Energy Conservation!"

- Make a transparency of the pie chart below. Display this transparency and share its information with your students. Ask students to identify the source(s) of energy used at the power plant that supplies electricity to their homes and the school. Then have each student make two pie charts: one showing his predictions for what this chart will look like in 50 years and the second, in 100 years. Have the student write a brief paragraph explaining his predictions.

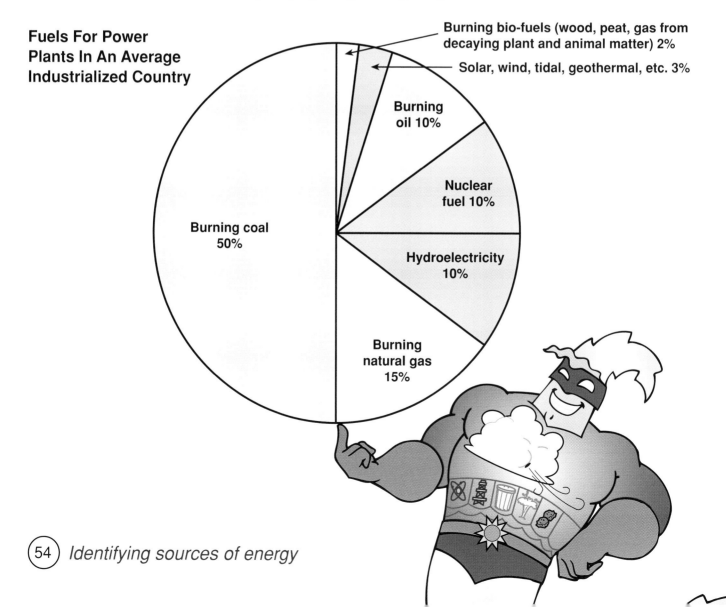

Fuels For Power Plants In An Average Industrialized Country

Burning bio-fuels (wood, peat, gas from decaying plant and animal matter) 2%

Solar, wind, tidal, geothermal, etc. 3%

Burning oil 10%

Nuclear fuel 10%

Hydroelectricity 10%

Burning coal 50%

Burning natural gas 15%

What's The Attraction?

*Attract your students to the principles of magnetism
with this hands-on lesson!*

Skill: Identifying the principles of magnetic energy

Estimated Lesson Time: 45 minutes

Teacher Preparation:
1. Obtain two bar magnets and several other magnets of various shapes and sizes.
2. Select various metal and nonmetal classroom objects, such as keys, a filing cabinet, rubber bands, coins, a door, straight pins, paper clips, and plastic game pieces.
3. Make one copy of page 57 for each student.

Materials:
2 bar magnets
iron filings
paper
3 different-sized magnets, 1 sheet of paper, a small pile of paper clips, 1 pencil, and 1 ruler for each group of students
1 copy of page 57 for each student

Background Information:
Magnetism is the force that causes something to attract or repel something else. A magnet is usually made of iron or steel and attracts only magnetic materials (such as iron, steel, nickel, and cobalt). Magnets do not attract materials such as plastic, paper, wood, and certain metals such as aluminum, copper, tin, and lead.

A magnet has a magnetic field (an area around the magnet in which the force can be detected) and two poles, a north-seeking pole and a south-seeking pole. Also, a magnet is attracted to another magnet only if the two opposite poles are brought together (north and south). Two like poles repel or push each other away (north and north or south and south).

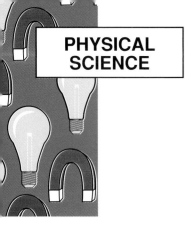

Introducing The Lesson:

Place a magnet on different objects around the room, such as a globe, blackboard, file cabinet, window, door, and student desk. Direct the students to note which objects the magnet sticks to and which objects the magnet does not stick to.

Steps:

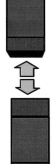

1. Ask your students why the magnet stuck only to certain objects. *(Students should be able to generalize that a magnet is attracted only to material with metal in it.)* Share the first paragraph of the Background Information on page 55 with your students.

2. Share the second paragraph of the Background Information with your students. Then show students two bar magnets with the north and south poles labeled. Next place one of the bar magnets on a lighted overhead projector. Sprinkle some iron filings on a sheet of white paper and place the paper on the bar magnet. Gently tap the paper with your finger. Ask students what they see happening. *(The iron filings curve around the poles.)* Explain to students that this is the magnetic field around the magnet.

3. Remove the labels from the two bar magnets; then put two ends of the magnets together. Ask students what they can figure out about the north and south poles based on the attraction of the magnets. *(If the ends attract, one is north and one is south. If the ends repel, they are either both north or both south.)*

4. Divide students into five or six groups. Distribute one copy of page 57 to each student. Provide each group with the materials listed on page 55. Instruct each group to complete each activity on the reproducible as directed.

5. Have each group present its findings to the class.

Pulling Power!

Magnetism: although its energy can't be seen or heard, its force is all around us. To find out more about this "magical" magnetic force, follow the directions for the experiment below.

Materials:

- 3 different-sized magnets
- small pile of paper clips
- sheet of paper
- pencil
- ruler

Procedure:

Step 1: Lay a sheet of paper on a flat surface. Put a paper clip on it and make a mark where you place the clip.

Step 2: Set a magnet several inches away from the paper clip. Slowly move the magnet toward the clip. Make a mark where the magnet was when it pulled the clip to itself. Measure and record the distance between the marks.

Step 3: Dip the magnet in a pile of paper clips. Note which part of the magnet picks up the most clips.

Step 4: Repeat Steps 1–3 with the remaining two magnets.

Observations:

1. What conclusions can you draw about the strength of each magnet?

_____

_____

2. Does the size of the magnet affect its strength?

_____

_____

3. What part of the magnet seems stronger? Is it the middle or the ends?

_____

_____

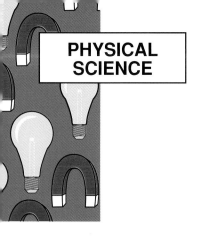
How To Extend The Lesson:

• Divide your students into groups of three. Supply each group with a shoebox, various paper and craft supplies, paper clips, glue, scissors, and several magnets. Direct each group to create a short animated skit about a favorite day, such as a day at the beach or a birthday party. Instruct the group to decorate the inside of the shoebox and create several cutouts to illustrate the story. Tell the group to fasten a paper clip to the back of each cutout and place the cutouts in the shoebox scene. Then have the group press a magnet against the back of the box behind the paper clip and let go of the cutout. Students will find that the force of the magnet keeps the cutouts from falling, and they will be able to share a *moving* story.

• Brainstorm with your students the many everyday uses of magnets. For example, magnets are used to post papers, keep doors and containers closed, and keep paper clips in place. Next challenge each student to think of a new and different way to use a magnet. Have the student draw, label, and color a picture of her new invention. Display the creations on a wall or bulletin board titled "Magnificent Magnets."

• Bury several metallic objects—such as paper clips, nails, tacks, and coins—in a container filled with sand. Place the container and a large magnet at a center. Invite each student to go to the center during free time. Challenge the student to find as many buried objects as possible using the magnet.

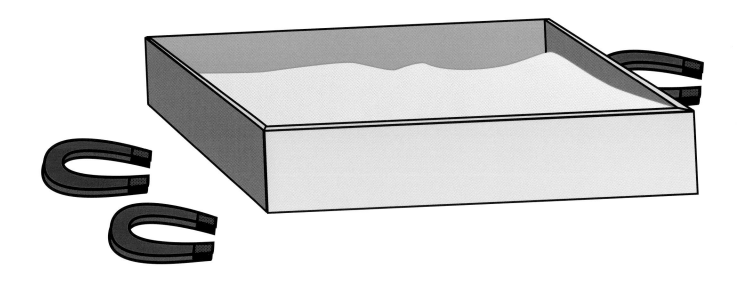

May The Forces Be With You!

Familiarize your students with the fantastic forces of push, pull, gravity, and friction with a lesson that's out of this world!

Skills: Identifying the forces of push, pull, gravity, and friction

Estimated Lesson Time: 1 hour

Teacher Preparation:
1. Copy the Background Information on this page onto a transparency or the chalkboard.
2. Gather a tennis (or another) ball and a book for a class demonstration. Also gather various items—such as a coin, a length of string, an eraser, and an empty plastic bottle or can—for each pair of students.
3. Duplicate a copy of page 61 for each pair of students.

Materials:
1 tennis (or another) ball and a book for a class demonstration
various items, such as a coin, a length of string, an eraser,
   and an empty plastic bottle or can for each pair of students
1 copy of page 61 for each pair of students

Background Information:
Forces are all around us. Forces allow us to breathe, throw a ball, or ride a bicycle.
- A *force* is a push or pull that makes an object move, or change direction or shape.
- *Push* is force pressed against something to make it move forward, outward, or upward.
- *Pull* is a force that moves something toward or nearer.
- *Gravity* is the earth's pulling force that makes things fall and gives things weight.
- *Friction* is a force that occurs when two objects rub against each other. It slows or stops moving objects.

Fantastic Facts About Force!
- The British scientist, Sir Isaac Newton, was able to describe the force of gravity after being hit on the head by a falling apple!
- In order to break through the earth's gravitational pull, rockets and space shuttles must reach speeds of 25,000 miles per hour!
- The longest recorded pull in a tug of war took place between Ireland and England during the World Championships in 1988. It lasted 24 minutes and 45 seconds!
- You would weigh almost three times as much on Jupiter as you weigh on Earth!
- Some racing cars travel so fast that when their breaks are put on, they glow red because of the friction between the disc pads on the discs!

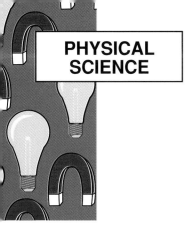

Introducing The Lesson:

Gather the tennis ball and the book. One at a time, throw the tennis ball into the air, pick up the book, roll the tennis ball along the floor, and drop the book on the floor. As you put each item into motion, direct your students to observe what type of movement is occurring.

Steps:

1. Explain to students that in order to move an object or put it into motion, you have to give it a *push* or a *pull*. Scientists call this push or pull a *force*. Share with your students the definitions of push and pull from the Background Information on page 59.

2. Ask students what type of movement occurred with each action—a push or a pull. *(throwing/pushing the ball into the air, picking up/pulling the book, rolling/pushing the ball along the floor, and dropping/pushing the book)*

3. Use the Background Information to discuss *gravity* and *friction*. Then throw the ball back up into the air. Ask students which force they think brings the ball back down. *(gravity)* Explain that without gravity, things would not stay on the ground. Next slowly roll the tennis ball along the floor. Ask students to identify which force makes the ball's speed decrease and eventually stop. *(friction)* Explain that the friction is caused by the floor pushing against the ball and reducing its movement or motion. Further explain that without friction, things would slip and slide away from each other.

4. Share the Fantastic Facts About Force on the bottom of page 59.

5. Pair students and provide each pair with various objects, such as a coin, a length of string, an eraser, and an empty plastic bottle or can. Direct each pair to use the objects to demonstrate each type of force. Have the group create a chart like the one shown to describe its force demonstrations.

6. Afterwards have each pair share its demonstrations and information on its chart with the class. Then give each pair a copy of page 61. Instruct the pair to follow the directions on the sheet for completing the activity.

Object(s)	Action	Force	Reason
coin	We rolled the coin along the floor.	push	Pushing the coin makes it move forward.
string	We used the string in a tug of war.	pull	Pulling the string brings it toward our bodies.
eraser	We threw it into the air.	push/gravity	We pushed the eraser upwards into the air, then gravity brought it back down.
coin, eraser, plastic bottle	We put the eraser and coin into the bottle. We rolled the bottle across the floor.	friction	The bottle slowed and stopped moving because of the friction caused by the objects rubbing against the bottle and the bottle rubbing against the floor.

May The Forces Be With You!

Force isn't just something found in science fiction movies—it's all around us! Forces allow us to breathe, walk, and even sing! Below is a list of everyday activities. Identify the force—*push, pull, gravity,* or *friction*—being demonstrated in each activity; then explain your answer. Write your answers in the spaces provided.

Activity	Force	Reason
1. bike skidding on road		
2. jumping off diving board		
3. skiing downhill		
4. shooting a basketball		
5. getting out of chair		
6. opening a can of soda		
7. brushing your hair		
8. riding a seesaw		
9. drinking out of a straw		
10. sliding into a baseball base		
11. tractor stopping in a muddy field		
12. opening a door		
13. sliding down a slide		
14. removing a nail from a wall		
15. paddling in a paddleboat		

Bonus Box: On the back of this sheet, list an example of four different forces found in your classroom.

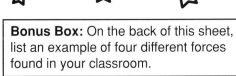

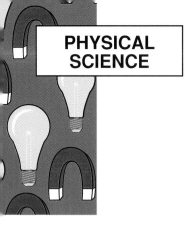

How To Extend The Lesson:

- Get your students to identify forces in action—firsthand—with this first-rate idea! On a sheet of loose-leaf paper, have each student create a chart like the one shown. Direct the student to observe her family, friends, and community members in action for one week. Have the student record her observations on the chart, identifying at least four different actions for each force—push, pull, gravity, and friction. Afterwards divide students into groups of four. Have group members share their findings with one another. Then have each group choose one example for each force to share with the class.

Date	Time	Persons Involved	Action	Force	Explanation
Nov. 2	4:25 P.M.	stock person at grocery store	stocking canned food	push and gravity	The stock person was putting the cans on the shelf (push) when all of a sudden, he knocked a can and they all started falling on the floor (gravity).

- Have your students create a class scrapbook of the forces found in their favorite activities. Provide each student with a sheet of drawing paper. Direct each student to bring in photographs of himself participating in various activities. Have the students bring in one photograph for each force. (Be sure to get parental permission for using the photos. Or, vary the activity by having each student search through magazines and newspapers for an example of each force.) Instruct the student to glue or tape each picture to the drawing paper and caption each picture with the name and explanation of the force. Afterwards, collect all the pages. Use two 9" x 12" sheets of construction paper as front and back covers. Use a hole puncher to make holes on the left side of the pages; then bind the pages together using yarn or brads. Finally have a student volunteer title and decorate the front cover. Display the scrapbook, having each student share his page.

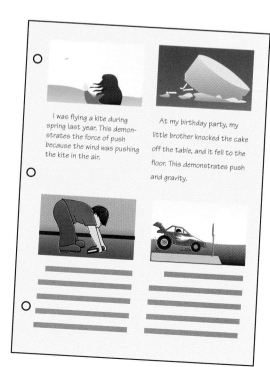

I was flying a kite during spring last year. This demonstrates the force of push because the wind was pushing the kite in the air.

At my birthday party, my little brother knocked the cake off the table, and it fell to the floor. This demonstrates push and gravity.

Seeing The Light

*Use this enlightening lesson to help your students understand how light
energy behaves and how its properties affect us.*

Skill: Recognizing and understanding the properties of light

Estimated Lesson Time: 1 hour

Teacher Preparation:
1. Duplicate one copy of page 65 for each student.
2. Gather the materials listed.

Materials For Demonstration:
cornstarch or baby powder
1 filmstrip projector, flashlight, or laser pen

Materials For Each Student:
1 piece of black construction paper
1 plastic sandwich bag
1 piece of waxed paper

Materials For Each Group Of Students:
2 large dictionaries
1 small flat mirror
2 white cards
1 black card
1 flashlight
1 clear drinking glass
1 penny
1 small paper plate
water

Background Information:
  Light is a form of energy known as *radiant energy*. That's because light *radiates*, or spreads out, in all directions from its source, such as a lightbulb or a star.
  Light travels in a straight line until something interrupts or changes its path. When light hits an object, the rays either pass through it, bounce off, or are absorbed by it. Light rays that bounce back are called *reflected light*. The image that is created when light reflects is called a *reflection*. Although many objects can reflect light, flat, shiny surfaces produce the best reflections. When light bends, it is known as *refracted light*. As light passes through two different substances of different densities, the speed of light changes. This causes the light rays to change direction, producing the "bending" effect.
  Light energy can travel through some matter, depending on the properties of that matter. A material that allows almost all light to pass through it is described as *transparent*. When only a little light is allowed through, the object is considered *translucent*. A material that does not allow light to pass through is called *opaque*.

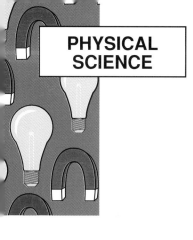

Introducing The Lesson:

To begin this lesson, turn off all the lights in the room and use a film-strip projector or a flashlight to project a beam of light. (A laser pen also works well if one is available.) Ask students if they can see the light beam *(only when it hits the wall)*. Sprinkle cornstarch or baby powder in the beam of the light. Ask students what they see now *(light traveling in a straight line)*. Explain to students that what they are actually seeing is light coming out of the light source and bouncing off the powder, then into their eyes.

Steps:

1. Explain to students that they will now be testing the movement of light through different materials.

2. Give each student a plastic sandwich bag, a piece of waxed paper, and a piece of black construction paper.

3. Have the student hold, one at a time, the plastic sandwich bag, the waxed paper, and the black paper in front of one of his eyes. Instruct him to look through the materials and observe any differences in how objects appear in the room.

4. Share the Background Information on page 63 with your students. Write the terms *translucent, transparent,* and *opaque* on the board. Discuss these terms with students. Have a student volunteer label each object from Step 3 as translucent, transparent, or opaque. *(plastic sandwich bag = transparent; waxed paper = translucent; black paper = opaque)*

5. Divide your class into groups of four students. Give each student a copy of page 65; then provide each group with the materials listed on the reproducible.

6. Instruct each group to complete the reproducible as directed.

Fascinating Facts

- Light travels at 186,000 miles per second. If properly directed, it could go all the way around the earth more than seven times in just one second!
- The brightest light from a lighthouse in Britain is on Stumble Head in Wales. The light is equal to six million candles!
- A rainbow is made by light falling on drops of water suspended in air shortly after a rain. One legend states that a rainbow is the bridge between heaven and earth.

Reflection Inspection

Leonardo the Lightning Bug needs you to help him inspect how light can be reflected. Follow the steps below to complete this activity.

Materials: 2 large dictionaries, 1 small flat mirror, 2 white cards, 1 black card, flashlight

Procedure & Observations:

1. Stand the books binding to binding. Prop the mirror against one book and one of the white cards against the other book as shown.

2. Turn out the lights. Shine the flashlight into the mirror so that the light bounces onto the card. Describe the brightness of the light on the card.

   _____

   _____

3. Replace the mirror with the other white card and repeat steps 1–2.

   Is the reflected light on the card as bright? _____

4. Replace one of the white cards with a black card. Bounce the beam off the black card onto the white card. Compare the amount of light reflected from the three different materials.

   _____

   _____

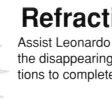

Refraction In Action

Assist Leonardo in solving the mystery of the disappearing penny. Follow the directions to complete the activity below.

Materials:

1 clear drinking glass   1 small paper plate
1 penny   water

Procedure & Observations:

1. Place the penny under the empty drinking glass. Place the small plate on top of the glass. Look inside the glass from all sides. Can you see the penny from every angle?

   _____

2. Have a partner stand opposite you on the other side of the glass. Have him lift the plate and slowly fill the glass with water. While the glass is being filled, keep your eyes on the penny. What happens to the penny? Why?

   _____

   _____

   _____

3. Switch places with your partner and repeat the activity.

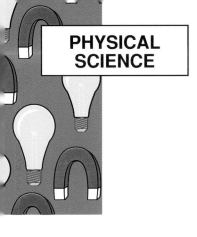

How To Extend The Lesson:

- Give your students more practice with reflection by participating in a little mirror magic. Ask students the following questions: "Have you ever seen the writing on the front of an ambulance?" and "Why do you think it is written this way?" Write the word "Ambulance" backward on the board. Invite a student volunteer to use a mirror to read the word. Next have students practice writing words backward. Pair each student with a partner. Have each student compose a message that is written backward on a sheet of white paper. Have partners exchange papers and use mirrors to read the messages.

- Provide each student with a large, shiny spoon. Have the student hold the spoon so that the front of the spoon is facing him. Next have the student turn the spoon around and look at his reflection again. Instruct each student to compare the images that he saw in the spoon. Have him research to find out about *convex* and *concave* lenses; then have him write a paragraph describing the differences in the two, using the spoon as an example.

- Have students make their own magnifiers with the following activity. Provide each student with a sheet of thin, clear plastic, a piece of newspaper, an eyedropper, and water. Have the student begin by placing the plastic over some small letters on the piece of newsprint. Then have him use the eyedropper to place a single drop of water on the plastic. Ask the student these questions: "Does the water do anything to the letters?", "What?", "Why?" Have the student compare the drop of water to a magnifying lens. Ask him, "What do magnifying lenses and water do to light?" Have him try changing the size of the drop of water to discover if the amount of magnification will change.

Leonardo da Vinci, a famous artist and scientist, wrote some of his notes in mirror writing to keep his discoveries secret!

Strike Up The Band!

From the buzzing of an alarm clock to the roar of traffic, sound surrounds us all the time. Explore this "resounding" form of energy with the following hands-on lesson.

Skill: Identifying how sound is created and how it travels through different mediums

Estimated Lesson Time: 45 minutes

Teacher Preparation:
1. Duplicate one copy of page 69 for each pair of students.
2. Gather shoeboxes (one per group) for the "Pitch Control" activity.

Materials For Each Pair Of Students:
1 ruler
3 rubber bands of various widths
2 pencils
1 shoebox or other rectangular box

Background Information:
Sound is a form of energy. All the sounds that we hear have one thing in common: each one is caused by the vibrations of an object. These vibrations can be passed from one molecule of a gas, liquid, or solid to the next. When these vibrations reach the ear, the brain interprets them as sounds. Sound waves must travel through a medium. If no medium is present, there is no sound. In general, sound travels faster through solids and liquids than through gases. Sounds can be described in the following ways:

- **frequency**—the number of vibrations made by an object per second
- **pitch**—the degree of highness or lowness of a sound
- **intensity**—relates to the amount of energy flowing in sound waves
- **loudness**—refers to how strong a sound seems when it strikes the ear
- **quality**—also known as *timbre;* the difference between sounds of the same frequency and intensity produced by different musical instruments

Identifying how sound is created and how it travels 67

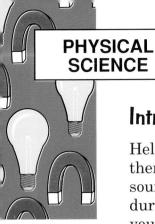

Introducing The Lesson:

Help students become more aware of the sounds that surround them by asking them to be completely quiet for one minute and listen intently to all surrounding sounds. After the minute expires, have each student list all the sounds he heard during the minute. Have students discuss their observations. Then ask, "Why do you normally not hear some of these particular sounds?", "Which sounds were important to hear?", "Which sounds were pleasant?", and "Which were unpleasant?"

Steps:

1. Explain to students that every sound they hear is produced by the vibrations of some object. Further explain that although many of the sounds we hear travel through the air, sound can move through any material.

2. Instruct each student to lightly tap on his desktop with his fingernail. Then have him place his ear to the desktop and tap again. Have a student volunteer describe the difference in the two taps. *(The tapping sound will seem much louder with his ear to the table.)*

3. Discuss the following points: What medium did the sound travel through with the first tap? *(air)* The second tap? *(wood, or a solid)* What can be concluded about the travel of sound? *(Sound travels faster through solids than through air.)*

4. Share the Background Information on page 67 with your students. Write each term on an overhead transparency or a chalkboard as you discuss it. Also read "Did You Know That...?" at the bottom of this page.

5. Divide the students into pairs. Provide each pair with one copy of page 69 and the materials listed on page 67.

6. Afterward, discuss the outcomes and student responses for each activity.

Did You Know That...?

- Compared with its speed through air, sound travels about 4 times faster through water and about 15 times faster through steel!
- The speed of sound is much slower than the speed of light. As a result, we see the flash of lightning during a storm before we hear the roar of thunder.
- A plane flying faster than the speed of sound, such as the space shuttle upon reentry into the earth's atmosphere, will create a loud noise called a *sonic boom*.
- Doctors can diagnose brain tumors, gallstones, liver diseases, and other disorders with *ultrasound*, sound with frequencies above the range of human hearing.
- Sound is absent in outer space, because there is no matter to be vibrated!

♫ ♩ ♪ ♫ ♩ ♪ ♫ ♩ Rubber-Band Banjo ♫ ♩ ♪ ♫ ♩ ♪ ♫ ♩

Make a little music with a rubber-band banjo by following the
procedure below.

Materials: 2 pencils, 1 ruler, 1 rubber band

Procedure & Observations:

1. Stretch the rubber band the length of the ruler.

2. Place a pencil under the rubber band at each end of the ruler.

3. Pluck the rubber band. Record what you see and hear when you pluck

   the rubber band. _____
   Does the rubber band make sound when it is not vibrating? Explain.

   _____

4. Press your finger at different points along the rubber band, plucking it each time.
   Write a description of the sounds produced each time you press the band and pluck.

   _____

   _____

   _____

♫ ♩ ♪ ♫ ♩ ♪ ♫ ♩ ♪ Pitch Control ♫ ♩ ♪ ♫ ♩ ♪ ♫ ♩ ♪

What makes one sound different from another? Follow the directions below to find out.

Materials: 3 rubber bands of various widths, 1 shoebox, 1 pencil

Procedure:

1. Stretch the three rubber bands around the box.

2. Write your predictions of how the pitch will differ when each of the three rubber bands is
   plucked.

3. Pluck each rubber band.

4. Twist the pencil near the end of one of the rubber bands and then pluck the rubber band.

Observations:

1. How did the pitch differ when you plucked each rubber band? _____

   _____

2. What happened when you twisted a pencil near the end of the rubber band and then plucked

   it? _____

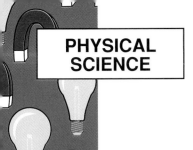

How To Extend The Lesson:

- Teach your students how to make beautiful music with a straw kazoo! Have them follow the steps below.

Materials For Each Student:
1 drinking straw
scissors
1 small paper cup

Procedure:
1. Pinch one end of your straw between your thumb and forefinger.
2. Cut off the corners of the flattened end of the straw with scissors to form a point.
3. Place about three centimeters of the cut straw into your mouth.
4. Pressing down slightly with your lips, blow into the straw. (After some practice, sounds will come from the straws.)

Observations:
1. What can you do to change the pitch of your kazoo?
   (Students can change the length of the straw to change the pitch.)
2. What happens if you use a paper cup as a flared end for the instrument? How does this change the sound you hear?
   (The flared cup will act as an amplifier, and the sound will be louder.)

- Many school cafeterias are noisy places, in part because they have few sound-absorbing materials built in. Have students list ways a cafeteria could be made a quieter place. *(Divide the cafeteria into smaller rooms by using sound-absorbing fabric partitions; hang school banners on the walls; cushion the chairs; "carpet" the floor with artificial grass.)* Record students' ideas on the chalkboard. Then have students write letters to the principal asking him to make changes in the cafeteria to provide a more pleasant dining experience for the children.

- Discover how well your students know their classmates with this activity. Select one student volunteer. Blindfold the student. Choose a few students to speak to the blindfolded student in normal voices. Can she identify who is speaking? Next have several different students speak to the blindfolded student in whispers. Can she identify who is speaking now? Why is it more difficult to identify students whispering than those speaking in normal voices? *(Students who whisper are harder to detect because the individual characteristics of their voices are missing.)*

It's Going To Blow!

Help your students understand the awesome power and wonder of volcanoes with the following activity.

Skill: Researching the different types and classes of volcanoes

Estimated Lesson Time: 1 hour

Teacher Preparation:
1. Make one copy of page 73 for each team of students.
2. Gather reference materials on volcanoes (see list of volcanoes on page 74).
3. Post a world map on a bulletin board.

Materials For Each Team Of Students:
1 copy of page 73
reference materials on volcanoes
2 pushpins
1 length of yarn

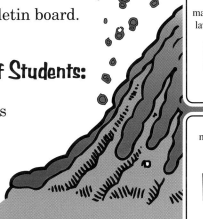

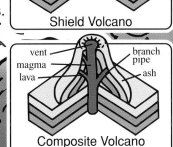

vent — gentle shape of basaltic lava flow
magma

Shield Volcano

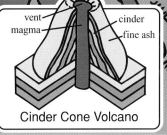

vent — branch pipe
magma
lava — ash

Composite Volcano

vent — cinder
magma — fine ash

Cinder Cone Volcano

Background Information:

The word *volcano* comes from the Roman god of fire, *Vulcan*. The ancient Romans believed that a volcano was a hot forge where Vulcan made swords and armor for the other gods.

Most volcanoes are found where the earth's crust is weak. Scientists believe that volcanoes begin with *magma* or melted rock deep beneath the earth's crust. The melting rock creates a gas that mixes with the magma, causing it to rise. Pockets of this gas/magma mixture are formed in the earth's crust about two miles below the surface. Pressure begins to build as more and more magma fills these pockets. Eventually the magma is forced up through the crust. Once hot magma reaches the surface, it is called *lava*. This hot lava pours out onto the surface of the earth. When the lava cools, it hardens into rock.

More that 1,500 active volcanoes can be found on the earth. Many volcanoes are found in the Pacific Ring Of Fire, which circles most of the Pacific ocean.

Scientists classify volcanic activity by how often a volcano erupts. Volcanoes are classed into the following groups:

Active—a volcano that erupts constantly.

Intermittent—a volcano that erupts at regular periods.

Dormant—a volcano that has become inactive but not long enough to know if it will ever erupt again.

Extinct—a volcano that has been inactive since the beginning of recorded history.

Scientists have also divided volcanoes into the three main groups shown below.

Shield Volcano—broad, shallow cones made when free-flowing lava pours from the top and spreads widely.

Cinder Cone Volcano—very explosive, formed when mainly *tephra* (cinders) erupts from a vent, then falls back around the vent, forming a cone-shaped mountain.

Composite Volcano—formed when alternate layers of lava and tephra erupt from one central vent.

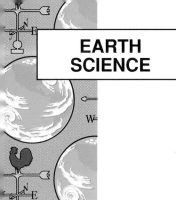
Introducing The Lesson:

Amaze your students with the following facts:

- Gases in the air we breathe come from volcanoes that erupted billions of years ago.
- The ground we walk on is partly made of molten rock from ancient volcanoes.
- All water on the earth began as steam from volcanoes.
- Much of the soil on the earth consists of volcanic ash, which makes it very rich in minerals.

Steps:

1. After reading the information above, continue to amaze your students by reading the Background Information at the bottom of page 71.
2. Next tell your students that they are going to work in teams of two or three to research an assigned volcano.
3. Distribute one copy of page 73 to each team of students. Assign each team a different volcano to research. (See list of suggested volcanoes on page 74.)
4. Make available to each team various reference materials on volcanoes.
5. Instruct each team to fill in the missing data on page 73 for its assigned volcano.
6. Have each team present its findings to the rest of the class. Then post a world map on a bulletin board and tack each team's "Mountains Of Fire" page around the map. Connect each page to the location of the appropriate volcano on the map using pushpins and lengths of yarn so that students can see the location of each volcano researched.

- Gases in the air we breathe come from volcanoes that erupted billions of years ago.
- The ground we walk on is partly made of molten rock from ancient volcanoes.
- All water on the earth began as steam from volcanoes.
- Much of the soil on earth consists of volcanic ash, which makes it very rich in minerals.

Mountains Of Fire

Directions: Your teacher will assign your research team a specific volcano to investigate. Use reference books, maps, and other sources of information to fill in the missing data below.

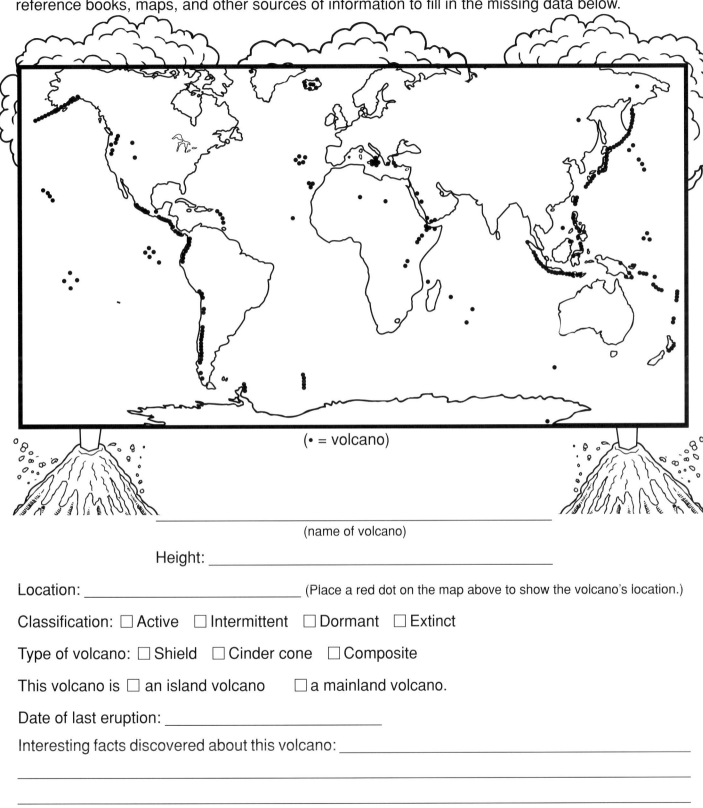

(• = volcano)

_____
(name of volcano)

Height: _____

Location: _____ (Place a red dot on the map above to show the volcano's location.)

Classification: ☐ Active ☐ Intermittent ☐ Dormant ☐ Extinct

Type of volcano: ☐ Shield ☐ Cinder cone ☐ Composite

This volcano is ☐ an island volcano ☐ a mainland volcano.

Date of last eruption: _____

Interesting facts discovered about this volcano: _____

_____

_____

_____

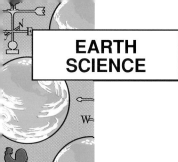
How To Extend The Lesson:

- Help your students experience volcanic activity by working in small groups to complete the experiment below. After each group has completed its experiment, have each group hypothesize why the eruption occurred. *(When you mix vinegar and baking soda, there is a chemical reaction. It makes carbon dioxide gas. Carbon dioxide makes bubbles, and the bubbles build up in the soda bottle. The bubbles take up space, and when there is no more room inside the bottle, the liquid comes out of the top of the volcano.)*

  Materials For Each Group:
  6 cups flour, 2 cups salt, 4 tablespoons cooking oil, 2 cups warm water, a 20-ounce plastic soda bottle, red flood coloring, liquid detergent, 2 tablespoons baking soda, vinegar, a funnel, a baking pan, newspaper

  Directions:
  1. Put some newspaper over the table and floor where you are working.
  2. Mix the flour, salt, oil, and warm water together. Mix it with your hands until the mixture is smooth. If it is too dry and crumbly, add a little more water.
  3. Stand the soda bottle in the middle of a baking pan. Press the dough up against and around the bottle. Shape the dough to look like a volcano. Do not cover or get dough inside the opening of the bottle.
  4. Mix together some warm water and a few drops of red food coloring. Using the funnel, pour the red water into the opening so the bottle is filled almost to the top. Dry the funnel.
  5. Add six drops of liquid detergent to the bottle. Pour the baking soda through the funnel. Next slowly pour some vinegar into the bottle.

- Share with your students the following books about volcanoes:
  The Magic School Bus Blows Its Top: A Book About Volcanoes by Joanna Cole (Scholastic Inc., 1996)
  Mountains And Volcanoes by Barbara Taylor (Kingfisher, 1993)
  Shake, Rattle, And Roll: The World's Most Amazing Natural Forces by Spencer Christian and Antonia Felix (John Wiley & Sons, Inc.; 1997)
  Volcano & Earthquake by Susanna Van Rose (Alfred A. Knopf, Inc.; 1992)
  Volcanoes & Earthquakes by Patricia Lauber (Scholastic Inc., 1991)
  Volcanoes: Earth's Inner Fire by Sally M. Walker (Carolrhoda Books, Inc.; 1994)

| Major Volcanoes And Their Locations ||
Volcano	Location
Mauna Loa	Hawaii
Mount Fuji	Japan
Mount Pinatubo	Philippines
Vesuvius	Italy
Mount Saint Helens	United States
Cotopaxi	Ecuador
Krakatau	Indonesia
El Misti	Peru
Hekla	Iceland
Kilimanjaro	Tanzania
Popocatepetl	Mexico

Are You Ready To Rock?

Get your students rockin' and rollin' with this cool lesson on rocks and minerals!

Skill: Classifying rocks and minerals

Estimated Lesson Time: 45 minutes

Teacher Preparation:

1. Duplicate one copy of page 77 for each student.
2. Have each group of students bring in five rock samples and the bottom portion of an egg carton. (See Step 3 on page 76.)

Materials:

1 copy of page 77 for each student
hammer
several rocks for classroom demonstration
5 rocks for each group
1 bottom portion of an egg carton for each group
1 unglazed ceramic tile for each group
1/4 cup vinegar for each group
1 eyedropper for each group
1 permanent marker for each group
scissors
stapler
safety goggles

Background Information:

Minerals are made up of simple chemical substances called *elements*. Some minerals are made up of a single element, and others are made up of more than one element.

Most *rocks* are made up of a combination of minerals. The eight major characteristics used to identify and classify rocks are:

- *Hardness*—measured using *Moh's Scale of Hardness,* which orders ten minerals from softest to hardest
- *Color*—the color of the rock
- *Streak*—the color that results when a rock is rubbed against something
- *Texture*—the size of the grains or crystals in the rock
- *Luster*—how the rock reflects light, which can be metallic, glassy, or dull
- *Cleavage*—how a rock breaks when hit by a hammer or another object
- *Chemical*—the chemical composition of the rock. For example, if a rock contains lime (calcium carbonate), it will fizz when acid is placed on it
- *Density*—the amount of matter in a unit volume of any substance

Introducing The Lesson:

Explain to students that rocks and minerals are identified and classified based on eight major characteristics. Point out that one of these characteristics is *cleavage*, or the way a rock sample breaks when hit by a hammer. Wearing safety goggles, demonstrate cleavage by breaking a rock sample with the hammer. Have students describe how the rock breaks. Then break another rock and have students compare the breakage.

Steps:

1. Explain that *hardness* is another characteristic used to identify and classify rocks and minerals. Geologists use a hardness scale invented by Friedrich Mohs of Germany. This scale orders ten minerals from softest to hardest, with talc being the softest mineral and diamond being the hardest. Share with students the following scale:

Hardness	Rock	Test Sample
1	talc	soft, greasy flakes on fingers
2	gypsum	scratched by fingernail
3	calcite	scratched slightly with penny
4	fluorite	scratched easily by knife
5	apatite	not scratched easily by knife
6	orthoclase	scratched by a file
7	quartz	scratches glass easily
8	topaz	scratches glass easily
9	corundum	scratches glass easily
10	diamond	scratches all other materials

2. Share with students the remaining characteristics used to identify and classify rocks found in the Background Information on page 75.

3. Divide your class into small groups. Provide each group with a ceramic tile, 1/4 cup of vinegar, a permanent marker, and an eyedropper. Have each group place five rock samples in the bottom of the egg carton, each in a different section. Direct each group to label each rock sample 1–5 by writing the appropriate numeral on the egg carton in permanent marker.

4. Distribute one copy of page 77 to each student. Have each group work together to further explore the characteristics of color, streak, texture, luster, and chemical composition of each rock sample.

Are You Ready To Rock?

Get jammin' to the beat of rocks and minerals with this cool activity!

Directions: Cut out the six notebook sheets below and place them in order with the cover on top. Staple the sheets together along the top edge. Observe the characteristics of the five rock samples; then record your information in the spaces provided.

ROCK LOG

Color is a rock's color.

Streak is the color that results when a rock is rubbed against something. To find the streak for your rock sample, rub it against the tile.

Texture describes the size of the grains or crystals in a rock. These grains are classified as coarse, fine, or nonexistent.

Luster refers to how the rock reflects light. A rock can have a metallic luster, a glassy luster, or it can be dull.

Chemical composition is the rock's chemical makeup. Use the eyedropper to place a small amount of vinegar on the rock sample. If it bubbles, the rock sample contains lime.

SKETCH | **SAMPLE 1**

COLOR _____

STREAK _____

TEXTURE
- ☐ coarse
- ☐ fine
- ☐ nonexistent

LUSTER
- ☐ dull
- ☐ glassy
- ☐ metallic

CHEMICAL
Does the rock contain lime?
- ☐ yes
- ☐ no

1

SKETCH | **SAMPLE 2**

COLOR _____

STREAK _____

TEXTURE
- ☐ coarse
- ☐ fine
- ☐ nonexistent

LUSTER
- ☐ dull
- ☐ glassy
- ☐ metallic

CHEMICAL
Does the rock contain lime?
- ☐ yes
- ☐ no

2

SKETCH | **SAMPLE 3**

COLOR _____

STREAK _____

TEXTURE
- ☐ coarse
- ☐ fine
- ☐ nonexistent

LUSTER
- ☐ dull
- ☐ glassy
- ☐ metallic

CHEMICAL
Does the rock contain lime?
- ☐ yes
- ☐ no

3

SKETCH | **SAMPLE 4**

COLOR _____

STREAK _____

TEXTURE
- ☐ coarse
- ☐ fine
- ☐ nonexistent

LUSTER
- ☐ dull
- ☐ glassy
- ☐ metallic

CHEMICAL
Does the rock contain lime?
- ☐ yes
- ☐ no

4

SKETCH | **SAMPLE 5**

COLOR _____

STREAK _____

TEXTURE
- ☐ coarse
- ☐ fine
- ☐ nonexistent

LUSTER
- ☐ dull
- ☐ glassy
- ☐ metallic

CHEMICAL
Does the rock contain lime?
- ☐ yes
- ☐ no

5

How To Extend The Lesson:

- Sponsor a Celebrity Rock Contest in your classroom. Begin by asking each student to bring in a rock. Provide an assortment of art supplies, such as yarn, movable craft eyes, and paint. Have each student decorate his rock to look like a well-known celebrity. Then have each student write a short biography about his celebrity. After the student shares his celebrity rock and biography with the rest of the class, have him display his creation on a table labeled "Celebrity Rock Hall Of Fame." Conclude the activity by asking a panel of judges to view the celebrity rocks, then select winners in categories, such as most creative, most interesting biography, and most realistic.

- Gather several reference guides on rocks and minerals from your school's media center. Challenge each student to collect several rock samples from the area around her home. Have the student place each sample in a plastic sandwich bag, then number each bag. Direct the student to record the number of each rock sample in a notebook along with information about the rock, such as the specific location and type of soil in which it was found. Then have students work in groups to identify the type of each rock sample.

- Explain to students that some minerals form regular, flat-sided shapes called *crystals*. Demonstrate how crystals form with the following two ideas:
  — Begin by mixing as much alum in a beaker of hot water as you can. Keep adding alum until no more will dissolve in the water. Place the beaker in a bed of crushed ice. Observe the mixture during the next few hours. Have students use magnifying glasses to view the newly formed crystals.
  — For a similar activity, fill a clear jar with very hot, but not boiling, water. Stir in salt or sugar until no more will dissolve in the water. Tie one end of a string to the center of a craft stick and the other end of the string to a button. Lower the button end of the string into the mixture, resting the craft stick on the mouth of the jar. Place the jar in a safe, draft-free location for a week or two. Have students use magnifying glasses to view the crystals.

Biome Buddies

Swing into the study of land biomes with this group booklet activity!

Skill: Examining the major land biomes and the plants and animals that live within each

Estimated Lesson Time: 45 minutes

Teacher Preparation:
Duplicate one copy of page 81 for each group of three or four students.

Materials:
(For each group of three or four students)
1 copy of page 81
4 sheets of 8 1/2" x 11" drawing paper cut in half
1 sheet of 9" x 12" construction paper
scissors
reference books
glue
access to a stapler

> There are more plant and animal species in the tropical rain forests than in all other biomes combined!

Background Information:

A *biome* is a plant and animal community that covers a large geographic area. A biome has the same general climate throughout the area. The eight major land biomes include the following:

- *Chaparral*—region with shrubs and small trees
- *Desert*—region with little plant life because of its scarce rainfall and dry soil
- *Grassland*—region covered with short or tall grass
- *Savanna*—grassland with scattered trees and shrubs
- *Temperate coniferous forest*—region with pinecone-bearing evergreen trees
- *Temperate deciduous forest*—region with trees that lose their leaves
- *Tropical rain forest*—region with a forest of tall trees, year-round warmth, and lots of rain
- *Tundra*—cold, dry region where trees cannot grow

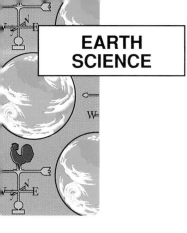

Introducing The Lesson:

Ask students to name some types of plants and animals that live around their homes. Then choose an animal that does not live in your area, and ask students if they have ever seen that animal around their homes. *(For example, if you live in the southeast United States, ask students if they have ever seen a polar bear in their community.)* Pose a similar question, this time choosing a plant.

Steps:

1. Question students as to why they haven't seen the types of plants and animals that you've mentioned in their area of the country.

2. Guide students to realize that plants and animals need particular living conditions, such as the appropriate climate and food supply, in order to survive.

3. Use the Background Information on page 79 to explain the term *biome* to your students. Point out that different biomes have varying rainfall amounts and temperatures. Tell students that these differences help determine which plants and animals survive in each biome.

4. Introduce the eight major biomes listed on page 79.

5. Divide your class into groups of three or four students. Provide each group with the materials listed on page 79 and access to reference materials.

6. Explain that page 81 contains some information on each of the eight biomes. Challenge the group to use reference materials to find and write two more general facts about each biome: one about the plant life and the other about the animal life. Have the group record these facts on the lines provided on each card.

7. Direct the group to cut apart the cards and glue each onto a different half-sheet of drawing paper.

8. Have the group draw on each paper at least one plant and one animal that live in that particular biome.

9. Instruct each group to bind its papers into a booklet by placing the pages inside a folded sheet of construction paper titled "Biome Buddies" and stapling along the folded edge.

10. Place the completed booklets in a science center.

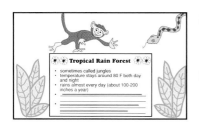

Grassland

- deep and rich soil
- averages 10–40 inches of rainfall a year
- _____
  _____
  _____
- _____
  _____
  _____

Tundra

- very cold, dry region where trees cannot grow
- region lies on top of a layer of ice that never melts
- receives only about 4–6 inches of precipitation a year
- _____
  _____
  _____
- _____
  _____
  _____

Coniferous Forest

- sometimes called a _needle-leaf forest_
- mild winters and heavy rainfall in coastal areas
- cool, moist mountain slopes
- _____
  _____
  _____
- _____
  _____
  _____

Deciduous Forest

- has four distinct seasons
- has rich, moist soil
- averages about 40 inches of rain each year
- _____
  _____
  _____
- _____
  _____
  _____

SAVANNA

- long dry season
- warm temperatures
- _____
  _____
  _____
- _____
  _____
  _____

Tropical Rain Forest

- sometimes called _jungles_
- temperature stays around 80°F both day and night
- rains almost every day (about 100–200 inches a year)
- _____
  _____
  _____
- _____
  _____
  _____

DESERT

- extremely hot temperatures during the days and cool, even freezing, nights
- less than 10 inches of rain per year
- _____
  _____
  _____
- _____
  _____
  _____

Chaparral

- coastal biome sometimes called _scrubland_
- cool and moist in winter; hot and dry in summer
- averages around 10 inches of rain a year
- _____
  _____
  _____
- _____
  _____
  _____

81

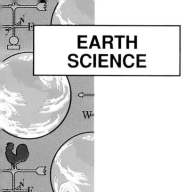

How To Extend The Lesson:

- Direct each student to choose one of the biomes discussed in this lesson and write a story about living in that biome. Have the student write the final copy of his story on a cut-out shape of a plant or animal that lives in that particular biome. Post these completed writings on a bulletin board titled "Life In The Biomes."

- Divide your students into pairs. Provide each pair with a large outline map of the world. Challenge each pair to use reference materials to label its map with the locations of the eight biomes. Have each pair include a legend or map key on its map.

- Assign each student a different biome. Give the student one 5" x 8" unlined index card and either colored pencils or crayons. On one side of his card, instruct the student to create a postcard illustration of his assigned biome. On the other side of the card, have him write the name of his assigned biome and a brief description of what he illustrated on the front of the card. Use a pushpin to display the illustrated side of each postcard on a bulletin board. Invite students to visit this board and identify the biome that is represented on each card. To reveal the correct answers, simply have students flip the cards over.

Tropical Rain Forest

The toucan lives in the canopy level of the rain forest. At this level the branches of trees grow close together, forming an umbrella over the forest.

Reduce, Reuse, Recycle

Inspire students to take part in cleaning up the environment with the following activities!

Skill: Recognizing the importance of conserving natural resources and protecting the environment

Estimated Lesson Time: 45 minutes

Teacher Preparation:

1. Gather a variety of clean, empty containers made of paper, plastic, aluminum, and glass.
2. Duplicate one copy of page 85 for each student.

Materials:

clean, empty containers made of paper, plastic, aluminum, and glass
chart paper
marker
1 copy of page 85 for each student

Background Information:

People have an enormous impact on their environment. Each day the population of the world continues to grow, creating more pollution, endangering more plants and animals, and consuming more of our natural resources. To prevent further damage to the environment, people must learn to *conserve,* or preserve by limiting the use of natural resources and producing less waste.

One way to preserve our planet is through *recycling.* Recycling helps conserve our natural resources by creating less garbage and using old products to make new products. Paper, plastic, glass, aluminum, and several other materials can all be recycled into new products.

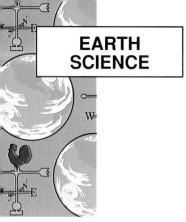

Introducing The Lesson:

Show your students several empty containers made of paper, plastic, aluminum, and glass. Ask your students what the objects have in common. *(They are all made of recyclable materials.)*

Steps:

1. Share the Background Information on page 83 with your students. Then ask them to think of ways the containers above can be recycled or reused. Encourage creative answers. For example, plastic or paper containers can be reused to store other materials, or they can be made into other items, such as bird feeders, baskets, or pencil holders.

2. Explain to students that we need to recycle to reduce the amount of natural resources used and the amount of *pollution* produced. Pollution is damage to the environment (land, water, air, plants, and animals) caused by trash and other harmful substances. Have students give specific examples of various pollutants, such as litter on the streets and chemicals from factories being dumped into waterways. Then ask your students who they feel are the main producers of pollution *(humans);* then ask students to name who are the most able to do something about pollution *(humans).*

3. Divide students into groups of four. Direct each group to brainstorm ways people can preserve natural resources and recycle materials at home and at school *(use both sides of a piece of paper, turn off lights when not in use, pack lunches in reusable containers).* Then, as each group shares its list with the class, compile the information by recording the group's response on a large sheet of chart paper. Title the chart "Planet-Pleasing Actions" and display it in a prominent spot in the room.

4. Distribute one copy of page 85 to each student. Challenge the student to become a "record-breaking planet pleaser." Have the student record her top 20 planet-pleasing actions from the class list and then record how often she completes one of the actions as directed on the reproducible.

Become A Record-Breaking Planet Pleaser!

Recycling, picking up trash, conserving water, saving energy, and protecting our environment are all ways we can keep our planet healthy and strong. So, how can you become part of the action? Beside the numbers below, record your top 20 "planet-pleasing actions," such as turning off unneeded lights, recycling newspapers, and picking up litter. Keep your list in a special place. Then, any time you complete one of the actions, record that action's number in one of the circles. Go for a gold record and fill in every circle.

Top 20 Planet Pleasers

1. _____
2. _____
3. _____
4. _____
5. _____
6. _____
7. _____
8. _____
9. _____
10. _____
11. _____
12. _____
13. _____
14. _____
15. _____
16. _____
17. _____
18. _____
19. _____
20. _____

How To Extend The Lesson:

- Obtain a copy of the book *50 Simple Things Kids Can Do To Save The Earth* by John Javna (Andrews and McMeel, 1990). The book, presented in a problem/solution format, empowers children by offering them valuable information and practical tips for preserving their world. Assign each student or group of students one of the topics in the book. Instruct each student or group to read the information, complete one of the projects, and then share the work with the class.

- Read a picture book such as *Just A Dream* by Chris Van Allsburg (Houghton Mifflin Company, 1990) or *The Lorax* by Dr. Seuss (Random House Books For Young Readers, 1971). After sharing one of the stories with your students, have students imagine what their futures may be like if people continue to abuse the environment. Then give each student a sheet of paper and crayons or colored pencils. Instruct the student to illustrate a scene from this imagined future. Display drawings on a wall or bulletin board titled "This Doesn't Have To Be Our Future!"

- Have each student write a letter to a national environmental organization such as the organizations listed below. In his letter, the student should express his concerns for the environment and request information on how he can help protect and preserve it.

Greenpeace International
1436 U Street NW
Washington, DC 20009

Keep America Beautiful
1010 Washington Blvd.
Stamford, CT 06901

Renew America
1400 16th Street NW
Suite 710
Washington, DC 20036

Clue In To Climate

Get your young "investi-gators" thinking critically about climate with this creative lesson.

Skill: Identifying factors that affect climate

Estimated Lesson Time: 1 hour

Teacher Preparation:
1. Obtain a large world map or globe.
2. Make one copy of page 89 for each student.

Materials:
weather forecast from local newspaper
large world map or globe
1 copy of page 89 for each student

The highest air temperature recorded was 58°C (136°F) in Libya, North Africa.

The lowest air temperature recorded was –88°C (–127°F) in Antarctica.

Background Information:
   Climate is the average weather in one place over a long period of time. Sunlight, temperature, precipitation, and wind are factors that affect climate in any given area. Temperature and precipitation are the most important factors affecting climate.
   Since the earth is tilted, the sun's rays strike it at different angles. The equator receives the most direct sunlight, and the poles receive the least direct sunlight. Air and water currents produced by the interaction between the sun's heating patterns and the earth's rotation and orbit are major factors in the distribution of heat and precipitation.

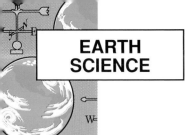
Introducing The Lesson:

Share with your students the day's weather forecast from a local newspaper. Point out the temperature, wind speed, precipitation, and amount of sunlight. Then have students describe the past week's weather conditions.

Steps:

1. Explain to students that *weather* is the condition of the air at any given time and place. *Climate* is the average weather in one place over a long period of time. Share the first paragraph from the Background Information on page 87. Then have students describe the climate of your area.

2. Have a student volunteer find the equator on a map or globe. Then have different volunteers find Venezuela, Egypt, and the North Pole. Guide students in describing the typical climate of each of these three areas *(Venezuela: lowland areas are warm and wet, higher elevations are cool and dry; Egypt: hot and dry; North Pole: cold and dry).*

3. Ask students whether there is a relationship between climate and location on the earth's surface *(yes).* Share the second paragraph from the Background Information. Emphasize that land areas nearest the equator generally receive the most sunlight, so these areas have higher temperatures. Land areas farther away from the equator receive less sunlight, so these areas have lower temperatures.

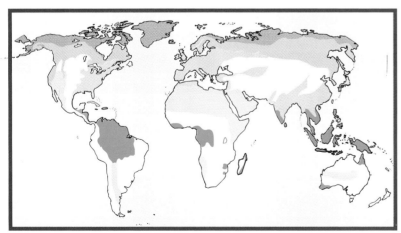

Biomes

⬛ Tundra   ▢ Temperate Forest   ▢ Grassland

▢ Taiga   ⬛ Tropical Rain Forest   ▢ Desert

4. Explain to students that scientists divide the earth into six major regions, called *biomes,* based on climate and plant and animal life. Use a map or globe and the diagram below to point out these regions to students.

5. Distribute one copy of page 89 to each student. Instruct students to complete the activity as directed; then have them share their findings about each biome's climate.

Name_____

Reading a graph

Climate Is The Key

The earth is divided into six major land regions called *biomes.* Each region's climate is different. The differences in climate affect the kind of plant and animal life found in each region.

Directions: Read the temperature and precipitation ranges on the graphs below. Use the information to answer the questions that follow. Record your answers on the back of this sheet.

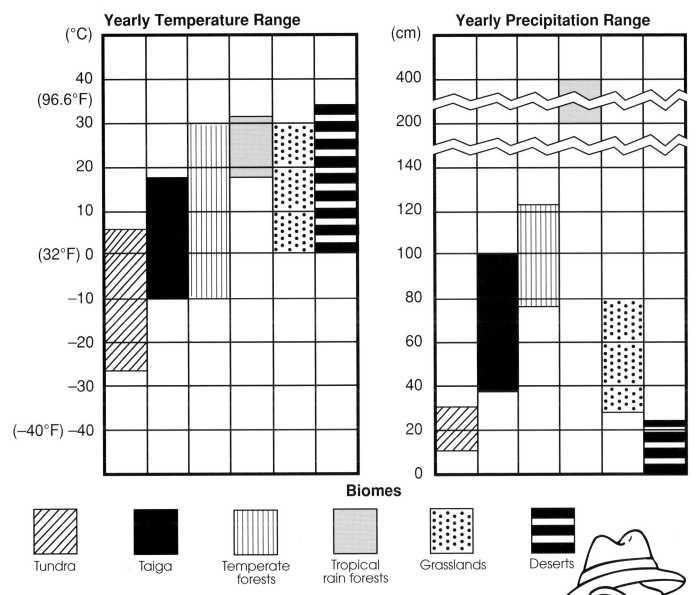

1. Which region has the widest temperature range?
2. Which region has the narrowest temperature range?
3. Which region has the coldest temperatures? Why do you think this is so?
4. Which region has the most precipitation in one year? Which has the least precipitation in one year?
5. If a city has very high temperatures and very little precipitation throughout the year, in which region is it most likely to belong?
6. Which region's temperature is about −10°C in the winter and about 17°C in the summer?
7. Use the graphs to describe the yearly climate of each region.
8. What do you think would happen to plants and animals living in a tropical rain forest if the climate changed to that of a tundra?

89

©1998 The Education Center, Inc. • *Lifesaver Lessons*™ • Grade 5 • TEC512 • Key p. 96

How To Extend The Lesson:

- Divide students into six groups and assign each group a different biome: tundra, taiga, temperate forest, tropical rain forest, grassland, or desert. Direct the group to research the climate and native plant and animal life of its assigned biome. Then have each group imagine it is a team of scientists exploring the area. Direct each group member to write a journal entry describing its area, including weather conditions and plant and animal life. Afterward, have each group share its journal entries with the rest of the class.

> With my long snout and sticky tongue, I find my food: tasty termites and ants that live in the undergrowth. The canopy of trees under which I live protects me from the heavy rains and strong sunlight.

anteater

tropical rain forest

- Place reference materials on the different biomes, a supply of 5" x 7" index cards, and markers or colored pencils at a center. Direct each student using the center to choose a biome to research. Then, on the front of an index card, have the student write a riddle about an animal living in that biome. Direct the student to include information about its physical characteristics, food requirements, and immediate habitat. On the back of the card, have the student write the name of the animal and the biome in which it lives. After each student completes a riddle, collect the cards. Post a different riddle each day, challenging students to guess the animal and its biome home.

- Pair students; then assign each pair a different U.S. city from the list shown. Direct each pair to use encyclopedias and atlases to research its city's average yearly weather conditions: sunlight, temperature, precipitation, and wind. Then have each pair use a newspaper to find that city's forecast. Have the pair decide whether the forecast is normal for that area based on its research. Afterward, have each pair share its findings and conclusion. Follow up the activity by having the class group the cities into regions based on similar climates.

Boston	Memphis
Chicago	Milwaukee
Charlotte	New York City
Denver	Orlando
Houston	San Francisco
Los Angeles	Seattle
New Orleans	St. Louis
Las Vegas	

Star Style

Add some sparkle to your classroom with this lesson on stars!

Skill: Comparing different types of stars

Estimated Lesson Time: 1 hour

Teacher Preparation:

1. Make a transparency of the diagram on page 92, or draw the diagram on the chalkboard.
2. Duplicate page 93 and the materials list and directions on page 94 for each student.
3. Gather the materials listed below for each student.

Materials:

1 blank transparency (optional)
1 copy of page 93 and 1 copy of the materials list and directions on page 94 for each student
one 9" x 12" sheet of white construction paper or tagboard, one 12" and five 6" lengths of yellow yarn, markers or colored pencils, scissors, and a hole puncher for each student

Background Information:

A star is a huge ball of glowing gas in the sky. Although there are trillions of stars, only about 6,000 can be seen from the earth without using a telescope. During the day, sunlight brightens the sky and keeps us from seeing the stars, so we can see them only at night when the sky is dark and clear. These stars are so far away that they look like tiny points of light in the sky, but they are actually quite large. Stars vary in size from the smaller *neutron* stars to *supergiants,* which are much larger than the sun. Stars also vary in color and brightness depending on their size and temperature. Colors vary—red, orange, yellow, white, or blue—and temperatures range from 5,000°F to 50,000°F.

Scientists predict that in about five billion years, our aging sun will swell into a red giant and ultimately eliminate life on Earth. Later, this giant will cool down into a cold, burned-out ember.

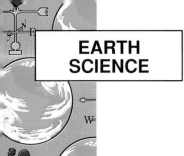
Introducing The Lesson:

Draw a large star on the chalkboard. Then have students tell you what words come to mind when they think of a star, such as *bright, far away, small, twinkling,* and *pointed.* Record their responses inside the star.

Steps:

1. You will probably need to explain to students that some of their ideas about stars are true, but others are not. Share the Background Information on page 91.

2. Discuss how scientists divide stars into five main groups based on size: *neutron stars, white dwarfs, dwarf stars, giants,* and *supergiants.* Display the star diagram transparency or chalkboard drawing. Have students use the diagram to compare the relative sizes of stars.

3. Point out to students that a star changes during its lifetime. For example, a large giant may grow into a huge supergiant, or if it uses up all its fuel, it may shrink down to a white dwarf. The greater a star's mass (the amount of matter of which it's made), the higher its temperature and brightness, and the faster it changes.

4. Distribute a copy of page 93 and a copy of the materials list and directions on page 94 to each student. Then distribute the materials listed on page 94 to each student. Read "The Story Of Stars" together as a class. Then guide each student in completing the activity as directed on page 94. Have several student volunteers share their descriptions; then display the resulting star groups by hanging them from the ceiling.

Our Sun
The sun is a medium-sized dwarf star. Its diameter is about 865,000 miles (109 times the diameter of the earth).

Star Groups

Neutron Stars
Diameter = about 12 miles.

White Dwarfs
Diameter = about 5,200 miles.

Dwarfs
Diameter = about one-tenth the sun's diameter to ten times the sun's diameter.

Giants
Diameter = about 10 to 100 times the sun's diameter.

Supergiants
Diameter = about 330 to 1,000 times the sun's diameter.

Note: Drawings are not to scale.

The Story Of Stars

When you look up into the night sky, stars look like tiny pinpoints of light. Actually, the smallest type of star is the size of a small city! Read the story below. Then follow the directions on page 94 to create your own star-studded mobile.

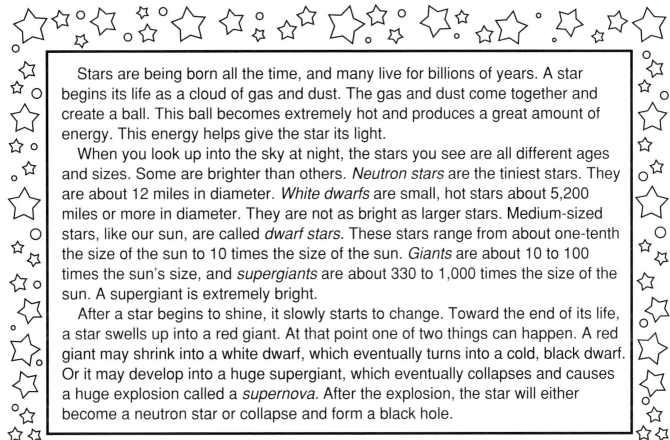

Stars are being born all the time, and many live for billions of years. A star begins its life as a cloud of gas and dust. The gas and dust come together and create a ball. This ball becomes extremely hot and produces a great amount of energy. This energy helps give the star its light.

When you look up into the sky at night, the stars you see are all different ages and sizes. Some are brighter than others. *Neutron stars* are the tiniest stars. They are about 12 miles in diameter. *White dwarfs* are small, hot stars about 5,200 miles or more in diameter. They are not as bright as larger stars. Medium-sized stars, like our sun, are called *dwarf stars.* These stars range from about one-tenth the size of the sun to 10 times the size of the sun. *Giants* are about 10 to 100 times the sun's size, and *supergiants* are about 330 to 1,000 times the size of the sun. A supergiant is extremely bright.

After a star begins to shine, it slowly starts to change. Toward the end of its life, a star swells up into a red giant. At that point one of two things can happen. A red giant may shrink into a white dwarf, which eventually turns into a cold, black dwarf. Or it may develop into a huge supergiant, which eventually collapses and causes a huge explosion called a *supernova.* After the explosion, the star will either become a neutron star or collapse and form a black hole.

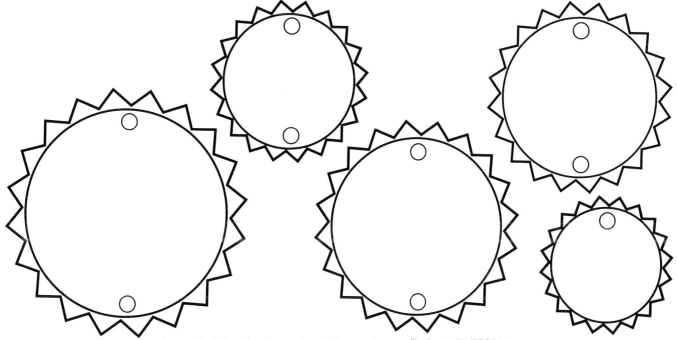

Note To The Teacher: Drawings are not to scale.

How To Extend The Lesson:

- Bring your study of the stars down to Earth with a sprinkle of grammar and writing. Remind students that an *adjective* tells more about a noun or pronoun. Then have each student choose a different letter of the alphabet. Challenge the student to use a dictionary to find adjectives beginning with her letter that could describe a star. (For example, adjectives for the letter *a* may include *ablaze, active, aged, alive, aloft,* and *astonishing.*) Afterward, post a large sheet of chart paper and have each student use a colorful marker to add her list to the paper. Follow up the activity by having students use the list of descriptive words in poems or paragraphs about stars.

- Guide students to recognize how stars throughout the universe are grouped by making glittering galaxies. Pair students. Provide each pair with a three-foot-square sheet of black bulletin-board paper, several sheets of newspaper, glue, and glitter. Direct the pair to research the different shapes of galaxies—such as *spiral, elliptical,* and *irregular.* Then have the pair draw each galaxy on its paper using glue. Before the glue dries, instruct the pair to sprinkle glitter over the glue. To reveal the galaxies, have the pair pour the excess glitter onto the sheets of newspaper. Hang the glittering galaxies around the classroom for all to enjoy.

Materials: five star patterns, a 9" x 12" sheet of white construction paper or tagboard, one 12" and five 6" lengths of yellow yarn, markers or colored pencils, scissors, and a hole puncher

Directions:
1. Cut out the star patterns on the bottom of page 93. Use the patterns to trace an outline of each star onto construction paper or tagboard. Cut out each new pattern.
2. Read the paragraphs at the top of page 93. Then write the name of a different type of star on each cutout. (Make sure each cutout matches the size of the star you are describing.) Color each cutout.
3. On the back of each cutout, write a sentence describing the star.
4. Punch the holes where shown.
5. Connect all the cutouts using lengths of yarn. Use the 12" piece for the top cutout.

Note To The Teacher: Use with "The Story Of Stars" on page 93.

Answer Keys

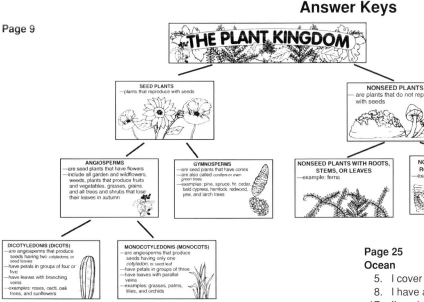

THE PLANT KINGDOM

SEED PLANTS
—plants that reproduce with seeds

NONSEED PLANTS
—are plants that do not reproduce with seeds

ANGIOSPERMS
—are seed plants that have flowers
—include all garden and wildflowers, weeds, plants that produce fruits and vegetables, grasses, grains, and all trees and shrubs that lose their leaves in autumn

GYMNOSPERMS
—are seed plants that have cones
—are also called conifers or ever-green trees
—examples: pine, spruce, fir, cedar, bald cypress, hemlock, redwood, yew, and larch trees

NONSEED PLANTS WITH ROOTS, STEMS, OR LEAVES
—example: ferns

NONSEED PLANTS WITHOUT ROOTS, STEMS, OR LEAVES
—example: mosses, fungi, and algae

DICOTYLEDONIS (DICOTS)
—are angiosperms that produce seeds having two cotyledons, or seed leaves
—have petals in groups of four or five
—have leaves with branching veins
—examples: roses, cacti, oak trees, and sunflowers

MONOCOTYLEDONIS (MONOCOTS)
—are angiosperms that produce seeds having only one cotyledon, or seed leaf
—have petals in groups of three
—have leaves with parallel veins
—examples: grasses, palms, lilies, and orchids

Page 13

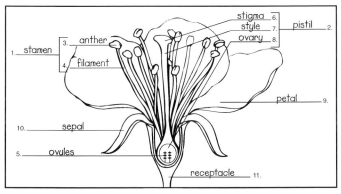

1. **stamen**—male reproductive part of a flower
2. **pistil**—female reproductive part of a flower
3. **anther**—produces pollen grains which develop sperm
4. **filament**—supports the anther
5. **ovules**—become the seeds when sperm cells fertilize the egg cells
6. **stigma**—sticky, pollen-receptive part of the pistil
7. **style**—the stalk of the pistil down which the pollen tube grows
8. **ovary**—contains the ovules and becomes the fruit
9. **petal**—colorful part of a flower used to attract insects and birds
10. **sepal**—protects the bud of a young flower
11. **receptacle**—reproductive parts of a plant are attached here

Page 17

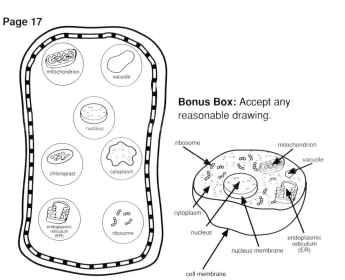

Bonus Box: Accept any reasonable drawing.

Page 21
Order of answers and interesting facts about animals will vary.

1. clam, invertebrate
2. turtle, vertebrate
3. amoeba, invertebrate
4. earthworm, invertebrate
5. dolphin, vertebrate
6. spider, invertebrate
7. cat, vertebrate
8. rabbit, vertebrate
9. jellyfish, invertebrate
10. starfish, invertebrate
11. crab, invertebrate
12. frog, vertebrate
13. fish, vertebrate
14. mouse, vertebrate
15. skunk, vertebrate

Page 25
Ocean
5. I cover about 70 percent of the earth's surface.
8. I have a variety of plants and animals that live at different depths.
17. I'm primarily salt water.
20. I include many species of fish and invertebrates.

Wetlands
12. I can be located near an ocean and contain salt water, or in forests and contain freshwater.
19. I provide homes for birds, fish, animals, and insects.
21. My areas contain permanent moisture: bogs, swamps, marshes, estuaries, ponds, lakes, and rivers.

Forest
6. I cover about 30 percent of the earth's land.
11. I provide homes for birds, insects, and animals, as well as sources of medicines.
13. I'm an area that helps absorb carbon dioxide, produce oxygen, and prevent erosion.
22. I contain tropical, temperate, coniferous, and deciduous trees.

Desert
3. I cover one-seventh of the earth's land surface, but because of environmental changes, that amount is increasing.
7. I receive less than ten inches of moisture a year.
14. I can be located in very cold or very warm climates.
18. Many plants and animals thrive in my hostile environment.

Tundra
4. My temperature range is from less than 0°C to never above 10°C.
15. The ground below my surface stays frozen all year.
16. I'm the name for the plains of the arctic circle.

Grassland
1. I'm a large expanse of land covered with tall grasses.
2. I'm also known as a prairie or savanna.
9. Most of my land in the United States has been plowed under and used for agricultural land.
10. I don't receive enough precipitation to support large trees.

Page 37
The scenes in each student's filmstrip should be pasted in the following order:
1. "Down The Food Tube"
2. Mouth
3. Pharynx
4. Esophagus
5. Stomach
6. Small Intestine
7. Large Intestine
8. "The End"

Page 41
1. True
2. False
3. False
4. False
5. True
6. True
7. True
8. True
9. False
10. False
11. False
12. True
13. True

SAYING NO: THE SMART WAY TO GO!

Answer Keys

Page 45
1. physical change
2. chemical change
3. chemical change
4. physical change
5. physical change
6. physical change
7. chemical change
8. physical change
9. chemical change

Page 49
1. conduction
2. convection
3. radiation
4. radiation
5. conduction
6. convection
7. radiation
8. convection
9. radiation
10. convection
11. radiation
12. conduction

Bonus Box: Answers will vary.

Page 57
1. Some magnets are stronger than others.
2. Some larger magnets may have a stronger pulling force.
3. More paper clips will collect at the poles of the magnet because the magnetic field is strongest there.

Page 61
Students' answers may vary. Accept reasonable responses.

	Force	Reason
1.	friction	bike tires rubbing against road
2.	push	pushing the body into the air
3.	gravity	gravity causing movement downhill
4.	push	pushing the ball upward
5.	push	pushing the body upward
6.	pull	pulling back top of can
7.	push and pull	pushing up brush and pulling it down
8.	push and gravity	pushing up the seesaw and gravity bringing it down
9.	pull	pulling the drink into the mouth
10.	friction	body rubbing against the ground
11.	friction	tractor tires gripping the mud
12.	pull or push	pulling the door toward the body or pushing it away
13.	gravity	gravity pulling the body down the slide
14.	pull	pulling the nail out of the wall toward the body
15.	push	pushing the pedals of the boat to make it move

Page 65
"Reflection Inspection"
   The mirror reflected almost all of the light from the flashlight. The white card reflected some light, but not as much as the mirror. The black card reflected very little light.

"Refraction In Action"
   The penny can be seen from every angle of the glass except from the very top (the paper plate shields the view) or when one's eyes are level with the bottom edge of the glass. The penny seems to rise in the water as the glass is being filled. When the water is poured into the glass, the light *refracts,* or changes direction, making it appear that the penny is moving.

Page 81
Answers may vary. Possible answers include:
Grassland
- large crops of grain are grown here
- home to many grazing animals and burrowing animals

Tundra
- low-growing plants and flowers live for a few months
- only a few animals (arctic foxes, polar bears, wolves) stay through the winter

Coniferous Forest
- mostly evergreen trees (including cedar, pine, and redwood)
- migratory birds and moose, elk, and deer

Deciduous Forest
- mostly trees that shed their leaves each year
- many animals hibernate through the winter when the trees are bare

Savanna
- grasses and sparse clumps of trees
- lions, zebras, giraffes

Tropical Rain Forest
- has about 400 different kinds of trees
- parrots, monkeys, lizards, snakes

Desert
- cacti and yucca; plant life is scarce
- many animals are *nocturnal:* active only at night when it's cool

Chaparral
- drought-resistant evergreen shrubs
- lizards, rodents, rabbits, and their predators find shelter under the shrubs

Page 89
1. A temperate forest has the widest temperature range.
2. A tropical rain forest has the narrowest temperature range.
3. A tundra has the coldest temperatures. It is located far from the equator.
4. A tropical rain forest has the most precipitation in one year; a desert has the least precipitation.
5. If a city has very high temperatures and very little precipitation throughout the year, it most likely belongs to the desert region.
6. A taiga's temperature is about −10°C in the winter and about 17°C in the summer.
7. *Accept reasonable responses.*
   Tundra: very cold temperatures, little precipitation
   Taiga: cold temperatures, fair amount of precipitation
   Temperate forest: some cold temperatures, fairly high precipitation
   Tropical rain forest: warm temperatures, very high precipitation
   Grassland: warm temperatures, little precipitation
   Desert: very warm temperatures, very little precipitation
8. *Accept reasonable responses.* If the climate in a tropical rain forest changed to that of a tundra, most plants and animals would probably die. Some animals might migrate to a more suitable climate, while others may eventually adapt to the new climate.